Road Map to Tomorrow

Road Map to Tomorrow

It's Easier to Get There If You Know
Where You're Going

By

John ***Morgan*** Mullen

Published in the United States
by eBooks2go, Inc.
1827 Walden Office Square, Suite 260, Schaumburg, IL 60173

ISBN-10: 1-5457-4242-1

ISBN-13: 978-1-5457-4242-6

Library of Congress Cataloging in Publication

Contents

Introduction

The speed of technological change is accelerating, and we are powerless to stop it. We have seen significant advancements in technology—from energy to transportation, from production to computers, from artificial intelligence to health care, and these advancements will only become more drastic.

What will the next thirty years look like? It's hard to say, but the objective of this book is to evaluate the direction that technology is heading so you can prepare for what lies ahead. Our world's productivity and efficiency are rapidly increasing, and it will change a great deal of what we currently know. We *must* find ways to adapt and adjust to the changes caused by these innovative disruptions to our jobs, our economy, and our lives. Our employment skills will change, our corporate structure will change, and the jobs that we have known for so long will no longer exist.

So ask yourself this question: "How do I prepare myself for a robotic future where the majority of the jobs as we know, do not even exist?"

Hopefully, the information contained here will assist you in finding the answer. *Road Map to Tomorrow* is intended to provide you with an invaluable edge needed for success by giving you direct information of where our world's technologies are heading. With a better understanding, you'll be able to identify what's in store for your future. The knowledge presented here provides more than merely an educated guess or a shot in the dark. It will deliver an outline of the world's future developments that, if prepared, could change your life.

The life-changing technological advancements changing our world today offer significant insight into our future tomorrow. In the book *Nirvana: Absolute Freedom,* Yogi Kanna states:

> Believing is not the same as knowing. Believing is secondhand knowledge, whereas knowing is firsthand experience. When your action comes from a level of belief and not firsthand knowledge, there is fear, doubt, and restlessness behind your action. When your action comes from a level of 'knowing,' there is conviction, certainty, and calm behind such action.[1]

The firsthand scientific knowledge presented here is not theory, but rather facts derived from in-depth research currently underway that provides the evidence required for "Future Proofing" your life and your career decisions.

We need to consider the challenges we will all face tomorrow in our rapidly changing world as well as the disruptive technologies we encounter today. My objective is looking forward with insight from the past while translating and adjusting to the inevitable changes of the future.

Learning from the past is an educational experience that will play a significant part in your future success. We must realize that we are not just competing against the person in the desk next to us but also against every person in our classroom, every scientist, manufacturer, and entrepreneur throughout the world. We are competing with every country in the world that, in many cases, have higher educational credentials with fewer political and economic constraints impeding progress and advancement. This is a wake-up call for us all. We are playing a new game, and we need to make sure we have all the tools necessary to succeed.

This book has been compiled utilizing personal research and a consortium of material found in books, magazines, websites, and online searches from reputable scientists who have discovered the technology to aid you in making successful and informed career and life decisions.

My objective is to inform, direct, inspire, shock, scare, and prepare. I aim to recommend but not dictate, to suggest but not require, and to gently provide options, as it's your future and yours alone to construct however you want. I do not have all the answers.

I do, however, believe the second-best thing is to know who does—or at least where to find them. The critical information in this book is provided by the experts and presented here are mostly in their words, not mine. You will also notice that the facts portrayed in some cases may vary slightly, as they are utilizing different data sources. Additionally, the time frames might be slightly different, therefore having different results. The material, articles, documents, and books that were utilized to assemble the data are highlighted throughout this book, as well as the recommended reading section, for further reference.

If you are debating what you need to study in college, if your current job is being eliminated, or if you are contemplating, "What do I want to do when I grow up?" then this book can provide you with great insight and options. This material will expose you to many areas that hopefully will coincide with your aptitude and interest. Additionally, you'll be provided with excellent guidelines to prepare you for success in your world by learning the potential high-demand sectors that will be the most relevant to your areas of study.

Life, not only allows but encourages elaborate and sophisticated "cheat sheets" and I'm here to help you develop yours. *Road Map to Tomorrow* offers excellent tips on technologies and the direction of our future world, talks about your possibilities, assists you in designing your plans, refining your passions and sets you on a course that guarantees success. Your future will become a lot easier to prepare for if you know the challenges, hurdles, and the opportunities beforehand. You have access to your very own cheat sheet for your professional and personal Life's Final Exams.

My intent for this book is to personally tour your future world so you can utilize this information to your best advantage. I am presenting the good, the bad, and the ugly, as life is never perfect or easy. My objective is not to sugarcoat or paint a rosy picture but to simply tell it like it is so you might prepare yourself for what lies ahead. I will help you identify areas of potential growth, assist you in learning about options available, and even help you find ways to research your inner-self to better understand and identify your greatest aptitudes and interests.

The road map for your future is incredibly important, as it will give you a peek into the journey you are currently taking or about to undertake.

Introduction

ix

*"If you don't know where you are going,
any road will get you there."*

—Lewis Carroll

Your journey over the next twenty-five to forty years, along with contributions from over one hundred scientific experts, will provide you with the insight into everything from computers to robots, from medical advancements to nanotechnology, from transportation to education, from employment to politics, and from entrepreneurial opportunities to love. As I like to say, "It's easier to get there if you know where you're going!"

I hope you enjoy the journey!

NOTE

I have attempted throughout this book to present extremely valuable information in various communication formats so that you can receive, enjoy, and better understand these future technologies. I have attempted to select recent articles and brief videos (under five to six minutes long) to provide condensed, current, and yet incredible information. You'll find hyperlinks in the recommended reading (Show and Tell) section at the end of this book that depicts what lies ahead for us all.

Technology Explosion

echnology is growing at a rapid and unpredictable rate. History has proven that our understanding of the future of technology is minuscule in comparison to the realities we will actually experience. The possibilities are limitless, and we can't fully understand the future capabilities of technology. To illustrate this point, here are past statements and predictions from some of the greatest minds the world has ever seen.

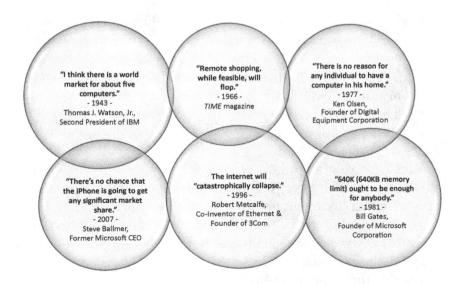

"I think there is a world market for about five computers."
- 1943 -
Thomas J. Watson, Jr.,
Second President of IBM

"Remote shopping, while feasible, will flop."
- 1966 -
TIME magazine

"There is no reason for any individual to have a computer in his home."
- 1977 -
Ken Olsen,
Founder of Digital Equipment Corporation

"There's no chance that the iPhone is going to get any significant market share."
- 2007 -
Steve Ballmer,
Former Microsoft CEO

The internet will "catastrophically collapse."
- 1996 -
Robert Metcalfe,
Co-Inventor of Ethernet & Founder of 3Com

"640K (640KB memory limit) ought to be enough for anybody."
- 1981 -
Bill Gates,
Founder of Microsoft Corporation

When some of the most famous scientific minds and inventors are this far off in their predictions and assumptions, it puts everything into perspective—there is no telling where technology will take us in the future.

The accelerating trends are taking place across a wide variety of technologies, including the internet, artificial intelligence, automation, advanced robotics, autonomous vehicles, renewable energy, and nanotechnology. These advancements are just beginning.

The World Economic Forum has an annual meeting to engage some of the top leaders in the world. Its focus is to shape the global, regional, and industry agendas. At the 2016 meeting, expert scientists from all around the world projected that we will experience a few of the following advancements and disruptions in the next ten to twenty-five years:

- 75 percent of universities around the world will go out of business.
- 50 percent of supermarkets will close their doors.
- Robots will be the soldiers of the future.
- DNA sequencing will personalize medicine.
- Autonomous cars will revolutionize and disrupt oil, auto, and insurance industries.
- 10 percent of the wealthiest industries will be "virtual corporations".
- Medical devises will scan and predict 95 percent of diseases.
- 70–80 percent of jobs will disappear over the next twenty years.
- 5 percent of consumer products will be produced with 3-D printing.
- The first 3D-printed liver transplants will take place.
- 10 percent of cars on US roads will be self-driven.[2]

Do I have your attention yet? Not all of these will happen, but with the rate that technology is advancing, many of these are entirely possible. In fact, we might not even be thinking big enough!

We've already seen its massive impact on the world, and as it continues to evolve exponentially and our predictions can only begin to explore the potential of technology in our world. Michael Baxter aptly makes this point in his book _iDisrupted._

> *"If we play it right, the result of the technological innovations that are afoot will be a kind of economic utopia...Technology does not have to replace us; it can enhance us."*[2]
>
> —Michael Baxter, *iDisrupted*

When significant innovation takes place, new markets are created and it has the potential to turn an existing and previously dominant market completely upside down. This is called disruptive innovation.

Subscription-based television, such as Netflix and Hulu, is an example of this. It's completely changing the television market. The cable market is diminishing, becoming less and less popular, especially among the younger generation, and it is entirely within reason to expect it to become obsolete in the near future.

Uber is another excellent example of disruptive innovation due to the ease and cost efficiency of its ride-hailing app that adversely impacted the taxi industry.

The disruptions caused by new technology have the power to destroy existing industries, eliminate jobs, and ultimately shift our economic markets. With the rapid technological changes taking place and much more to come, I am expecting that we will see and will be required to prepare for several more major market disruptions over the next twenty to twenty-five years.

Technologies That Will Disrupt Markets

Artificial Intelligence

Improvements to artificial intelligence and other machine learning are shifting the workforce from human-operated tasks to machine-operated tasks. Autonomous machines are now doing work that once seemed impossible for a machine to do. As improvements continue, autonomous machines will find ways to perform highly skilled tasks. Many jobs that have forever been performed by humans could become fully automated. This will completely change the job market and workforce as we know it.

Computers and Advanced Robotics

For years we have seen robots in the manufacturing field doing some of the difficult, grueling, and reasonably low-skilled jobs in production. However, recently we have seen significant advancements in the qualities of robots such as the intelligence, sensors, vision, and communication. This makes the potential of the work that robots can achieve, limitless.

Their abilities in manufacturing will continue to improve, meaning they can be given more responsibilities and even work alongside humans. We are also beginning to see their capabilities in industries other than production, such as service jobs, cleaning, and maintenance. They are even impacting the medical field with research, diagnostic skills, and robotic surgery. It will be exciting to see how computers and robotics continue to impact our world.

Genetic Modifications

According to Wikipedia, human genome sequencing is the ability to determine the sequence of the base pairs that make up human DNA.[3] This helps us to understand the makeup of diseases and mutations. Human genome sequencing initially took thirteen years at the cost of $2.7 billion.

Today, with rapid human genome sequencing using powerful computers, genetic variations can be specifically tested to understand what brings about specific traits and diseases. Now, this can be done in several hours at a relatively cheap cost, something that seemed impossible just a decade ago. As advancements continue, treatment of diseases will greatly improve. There is even the possibility we'll be able to customize and edit DNA, which could remove diseases altogether. These possibilities would have a huge impact on medicine, health care, and agriculture.

Autonomous Vehicles

Driverless cars are no longer just a science fiction concept. We now have the technology, and it will turn our transportation world upside down. Cars, trucks, aircraft, and watercraft can now be run entirely or partly autonomously. The technology that makes autonomous

Morgan

❖

4

vehicles possible is rapidly growing, so the advancements we've seen in recent years is likely nothing compared to what we are about to see in the years to come.

We've seen autonomous cars already make road transportation much safer, with driving assistance such as steering, braking, and collision avoidance. In the future, we will see other autonomous vehicles, such as trucks and drones, invade the trucking and shipping industries. This will significantly improve productivity and shift the market altogether.

Renewable Energy and Energy Storage

Solar, wind, water, and nuclear power are all examples of renewable energy. Not only are they renewable but they are also clean sources of energy, making them much better for our earth. As technology improves, accessing these sources of energy will become easier and cheaper, and because of the benefits of renewable energy, they will soon control a large portion of the energy market. Fossil fuel has long dominated this market, but we are quickly running out of it, and we have seen the harmful effects it has on our world, such as global warming. As renewable energy sources become more accessible, clean energy will begin to replace fossil fuel energy completely.

Energy storage allows for batteries and other systems to store energy for later use. Lithium-ion batteries are currently powering electric and hybrid vehicles. As the performance of Lithium-ion batteries increases and their price reduces, we should see electric cars become cost competitive with fuel-run cars. This will make electric vehicles available to a much larger market, not just the upper class as we have mostly seen up to this point. This is only one example, but the same concept follows with other sources of stored energy.

Industries that once dominated a market will become nonexistent, along with the jobs within the industry. With these and other potentially disruptive innovations on the horizon, we'll be required to adapt the way we live and work. But disruptive innovations are not bad. We have seen time and time again that innovation typically creates more jobs than it destroys. We are looking at incredible new technologies that will solve problems, make our lives easier and more efficient, and lower costs for consumers because of increased production efficiency. But nonetheless, change is frightening, and it

Technology Explosion

5

will require continuous adaptation in areas such as business, politics, health care, transportation, jobs, and nearly every aspect of our economy.

We aren't just interested in the potential technological advancements we'll be facing in the future. The reason we look at these predictions is to better understand how the world will change and how our lives as individuals will be impacted. We don't know exactly where technology will take us, but now that you see a glimpse of the potential impact, I hope you realize how important it is to try and prepare for this future world as best we can.

Many great career choices will be presented throughout this book with the hope of helping you find potential paths you can take in the ever-changing world. Not just potential jobs but fields of study and industries as well. Because who's to say these jobs will even still exist in the future? Regardless, this book is more about providing you a menu of options for you to consider so you might find what you are most passionate about.

Please understand I'm not here to lay out your life plan for you. That will be up to you, both now and over the course of your life. My goal is to gather facts, analyze and evaluate the scientific research performed by experts, and inform you of their findings so that you're able to see how these discoveries are anticipated to affect everything around us exponentially.

The information presented here is meant to assist you in making good career decisions and choosing your potential areas of interest. So prepare yourselves accordingly—study hard, find your passions, and pursue those areas with a road map and an informed mind.

The Intelligence of Artificial Intelligence

Artificial intelligence (AI) has proven itself to be the most incredible and powerful tool mankind has ever seen. No other technology is gaining more momentum, seeing more progress, or inciting more fear than the rise of intelligent machines. So what exactly is it? Let's break the two words up. *Artificial* is defined as something that does not occur naturally but rather is produced by human beings.[3] *Intelligence* is defined as the mental capacity to learn, reason, and understand.[4]

So what does it mean when we put these two words together? Well, if natural intelligence is the ability of the human mind to cognitively think, adapt, learn, reason, respond, problem solve, etc., then artificial intelligence is this same process occurring outside the human mind. Wikipedia defines *artificial intelligence* as intelligence exhibited by machines rather than humans. An intelligence that mimics the cognitive functions of a human mind, such as learning and problem solving.[5]

Most of us see and use artificial intelligence in our daily lives, with devices like Alexa and Siri. We ask a question or make a request, and the device intelligently responds to the best of its ability. Over the last several years, we have seen this intelligence improve drastically to become more cognitive and natural.

Even though the general understanding is that artificial intelligence is technically unnatural, the argument is that intelligence is intelligence no matter what form it takes, whether generated by a human, or by means like a computer or device. Look at what Albert Einstein had to say about intelligence.

> *"The measure of intelligence is the ability to change."*
>
> —Albert Einstein

Artificial intelligence is clearly a form of intelligence, and we are starting to see its ability to change and adapt. There is no doubt that machines will continue to improve in this area. A common belief is that as computer systems get smarter, they will become capable of examining themselves to make modifications to their software to improve their intelligence. In other words, they would be able to design their own hardware, removing any need for human intelligence at all.

It is unknown whether this is possible and just how intelligent these machines can eventually become, but there is the belief among many of the smartest people in the world who fear the possibilities of artificial intelligence. Can they develop a mind of their own? Can they create their own goals? Yes! However, we aren't exactly sure to what extent and how that will impact our future.

There are some earnest discussions taking place as to when artificial intelligence will surpass human intelligence, if it hasn't already. This is referred to as singularity. It could create a "runaway reaction" of self-improvement cycles, with each new and more intelligent generation appearing more and more rapidly, causing an intelligence explosion and resulting in a powerful superintelligence that would far surpass all human intelligence.

We are already seeing computer systems such as Watson and all its current relatives, (Siri, Alexa, and friends) not only having the ability to absorb information at unimaginable speeds with retentions that humans are incapable of but also be intelligent enough to ask clarifying questions to help find the appropriate answers. Furthermore, they have proven to be correct in more instances than human research.

AI has made great strides in recent years, and its current pace of breakthrough is stunning. We've seen crucial progress in fields such as medicine, where it has spurred breakthroughs in disease diagnosis and the development of treatment plans. It's given transportation new capabilities, such as self-driving vehicles, which we will discuss later. It's opened new opportunities in manufacturing, where it optimizes productions and can detect product defects. We're just now starting to scratch the surface of where AI can take us.

Machines have shown to be highly effective, exceeding human performance in most areas. Therefore, they are replacing the work of humans in many fields. For example, with machines having an increased role in manufacturing, human labor is no longer needed, which cuts down on jobs and reduces costs. As these machines continue to improve their ability to learn, respond, and adapt, they'll continue to replace the work currently performed by humans.

IBMs Watson is an example of an artificial intelligent system that is disrupting multiple industries, including bookkeeping and accounting. Call center agents respond to your call in a lifelike voice that can often be difficult to detect if you're speaking with a live agent or an intelligent system. In the future, even legal assistants will utilize intelligent systems. Virtual lawyers will be accessible as large law firms will begin to use intelligent agents to take on legal cases at a lower cost than traditional firms. This is just the tip of the iceberg.

While this is great for the world's overall efficiency, it will cut out many jobs people have always relied on. I think, when looking at the whole picture, our world will significantly benefit from the growth of artificial intelligence, but this will create new challenges that we have never dealt with. We must learn to adapt while looking for new solutions.

Artificial intelligence will only continue to improve with advancements in computers that will create faster data and more sophisticated algorithms. We're in the midst of a computing platform revolution that is primed to change every aspect of the world as we know it. Throughout this book, I will attempt to project how these

The Intelligence of Artificial Intelligence

advancements may affect our lives and how we can adjust to prepare for the future.

Examples of Jobs in Artificial Intelligence

Machine Learning Engineer
Research Scientist
Computer Vision Engineer

See more in Chapter 9, "Help Wanted"

Quantum Computing

"If GM had kept up with technology like the computer industry has, we would all be driving $25 cars that got 1,000 mpg."

—Bill Gates

Computers are powerful, and in the short time since they have been invented, they've completely changed our world. As we look to the future, we look for new and better ways a computer can make our lives more efficient and productive. The new Supercomputers are capable of speeds that exceed 200 Quadrillion calculations per second. They have named this supercomputer the "Verge" as it puts us on the verge of quantum computing, which is scary fast and puts us light years ahead of today.

The History of Computers

It's difficult to determine when the first computer was invented. The advancements in computers have been so drastic that it almost seems like a stretch to call the first computers *computers*. The original computers were purely mechanical devices that required the operator to set up the initial values of an elementary arithmetic operation and then manipulate the device to obtain the result. There were a number of inventors to receive credit for the development of the computers.

According to <u>Live Science</u>, Charles Babbage was the earliest in 1822. He conceived the concept of a computing device, but he never achieved the funding to actually put this vision into action. Then, in the 1940s, people such as Konrad Zuse, Alan Turing, Vincent Atanasoff, Cliff Berry, and Presper Eckert played significant roles in the development of computers.[4]

Centre for Computing History says that the first electronic programming computer, called Colossus, was designed by English engineer <u>Thomas *"Tommy"* Flowers</u>. This machine helped solve encrypted German messages during World War II. Without these machines, the war would have lasted much longer, and the Allies may have even lost. They would have been deprived of very valuable intelligence obtained from reading the encrypted messages between the Germans and their army command, such as intelligence regarding the D-day landings and the disposition of German troops in Normandy. Not only was this machine critical for the outcome of WWII but it also played a major role in the future of computer systems.[5]

As Wikipedia states, <u>computers continued to progress</u> through a series of breakthroughs, such as digital circuits, stored-program computers, miniaturized transistor computers, and integrated circuits, that caused digital computers to largely replace analog computers. Following developments such as the microprocessor, the cost of computers gradually lowered. By the 1990s, personal computers became common in industrialized countries and were then followed by mobile devices (laptops, smartphones, and tablets) in the 2000s.[6]

To give you an idea as to how far we've come, the original model designed by Barry/Atanasoff, occupied eighteen hundred square feet and weighed fifty tons, compared to today's smartphones, which have exponentially more capabilities and power while also fitting easily into our pockets.

The Internet

The development of the internet was originally funded by the US Department of Defense in 1960 with the development of the Advanced Research Projects Agency Network (ARPANET), an experimental computer network of technologies that became the technical foundation of the internet. Dozens of science and government agencies developed the internet in conjunction with the advancements in the computer industry. It provides us with immediate access to tremendous amounts of data and instant communication throughout every corner of our world, from business to politics, from social to medical, and from computers to education.

Patterns Leading to the Future

When comparing the processing power of various computers and devices from 1956 to present, the amount would equate to a trillionfold increase in performance over those six decades. At this current pace, it is predicted that by 2058 a computer's power will be that of one billion brains! We are rapidly moving into a world in which at least fifty billion devices will be connected to the web and each other globally. Stephen Lawson, senior US correspondent of IDG News Service, stated that " ... the amount of traffic on wireless networks will have multiplied by 88 times between 2010 and 2020, while wired access networks will grow about 10 times busier and wired core networks will see traffic multiply by eight times."[7]

Mobile technology will continue to evolve and will soon reach the next level. Millions around the world will be connected through mobile devices of all shapes and sizes. We have already begun to see this movement take place with the likes of Apple Watches and Google Glasses. It is absolutely mind-boggling to realize just how far technology can take us.

Research is currently being conducted to study ways of integrating computers with our minds. "We're trying to prove you can do interesting things with brain waves," said Intel research scientist Dean Pomerleau. "Eventually people may be willing to be more committed ... to brain implants. Imagine being able to surf the Web with the power of your thoughts."[8]

Quantum Computing

Research groups are currently working with brain-scanning devices to map blood flow in the brain. They have found that very similar patterns of blood flow appear for different individuals when looking at the same image. This means that with some refining and further advancements, computers may be able to understand what we are thinking and feeling based on the activity going on in our brains. For example, a British group announced they could determine where subjects were within a computer-generated virtual environment just by looking at the blood flow in their brains. There is still major room for improvement in this area, but something that the majority of us always assumed was impossible is now seemingly reachable.

Along this same line of biotechnology, even our vision will move into the future. Research has begun to create a contact lens-like computer screen as a wearable visual aid. In an article by Phys.org, Michele Nardelli states:

> Scientists from the University of South Australia's Future Industries Institute have successfully completed 'proof of concept' research on a polymer film coating that conducts electricity on a contact lens, with the potential to build miniature electrical circuits that are safe to be worn by a person. UniSA researcher from the FII, Associate Professor Drew Evans said the technology was a 'game changer' and could provide one of the safest methods to bring people and their smart devices closer together.[9]

If our vision is eventually connected to technology, essentially everything we do will be affected by technology. But is bringing people and their smart devices closer together really a good idea? Many would argue we already are becoming overly attached and too dependent to our devices. Of course, you can decide to take the contact lenses out, but most of us can't even leave home without our phones. Technology already plays a major role in our lives, and it's only going to increase as time goes on.

It's important to realize that research for the immediate future is far more reliable than researcher's projections for, say, twenty-five to forty years from now. Obviously, there are a lot more unknowns with things further down the line. That's not to say the projections are worthless. They can still be very insightful and even thought-provoking and they're driven by the facts we do have. But I need to reel it back a bit, so I don't jump from the biblical, ancient world of Moses straight into the futuristic world of *Star Trek*'s Doctor Spock. It's hard, if not impossible, to wrap our minds around some of the possibilities one hundred or even fifty years into the future.

Given the rapid rate of technological advancements, I wholeheartedly believe you need to design your future game plan utilizing the information and projections we are given. Form your life's plan and career aspirations with this data in mind. Not everything will fall into place; not everything will go according to plan. And not everything in these predictions will come true. But if you prepare yourself for the future, even the unexpected can't throw you off. You will find success in life when you become easily adaptable. Since change is happening at a greater rate than ever before, adaptability is a must.

Examples of Jobs in Computer Technologies

Software Engineer
Mobile App Developer
Video Game Designer

See more in Chapter 9, "Help Wanted"

Chapter

Robots are My Friends

What comes to mind when you think of a robot? Maybe it's the friendly R2-D2 from *Star Wars* or the mighty Optimus Prime from *Transformers*. Perhaps you think of a machine that follows the instructions of a human to make their life a little easier, or maybe you think of an intelligent machine that develops a mind of its own to outsmart the human race to rule the world. Whatever it is, all of us likely have a vision of what we believe robots to be, and the reality is, our understanding and preconceived perception of robots is probably wrong.

So what exactly is a robot? Robot Institute of America (RIA) defines a robot as "a programmable, mechanical device used in place of a person to perform dangerous or repetitive tasks with a high degree of accuracy."[10]

The first industrial robots were invented in the 1950s by George C. Devol. He called this invention "Unimate," short for "Universal Automation." He eventually partnered with businessman and engineer Joseph Engleberger, and together they formed Unimation, the world's first robotics company. They began to produce the robots, and in 1961 the first Unimate robotic arm was installed at a General Motors plant. This robotic arm helped speed up and maximize the production for General Motors. Soon other automotive companies, such as Chrysler and Ford Motor Company, followed suit and installed the industrial robots into their manufacturing facilities as well.[11]

Robots have come a long way since then, and as developments in technology and artificial intelligence progress, robots will continue to advance in their capabilities as well.

Dr. Jing Bing Zhang, Research Director of IDC Worldwide Robotics, published a report titled _IDC Unveils its Top 10 Predictions for Worldwide Robotics for 2017 and Beyond._ He highlights the key drivers for robotics and how these are likely to shape the development of technology in the next few years.

> Robotics will continue to accelerate innovation, thus disrupting and changing the paradigm of business operations in many industries. IDC expects to see stronger growth of robotics adoption outside the traditional manufacturing factory floor, including logistics, health, utilities and resources industries. [IDC] embrace(s) and assess(es) how robotics can sharpen their company's competitive edge by improving quality, increasing operational productivity and agility, and enhancing experiences of all stakeholders.[12]

All areas of technology are connected, and when one specific area improves, there will be ripple effects felt across the entire field.

Robotic engineers are designing the next generation of robots to look, feel, and act more humanlike, making it easier for us to warm up to a cold machine. Realistic-looking hair and skin embedded with sensors will allow robots to react naturally in their environment. For example, a robot that senses your touch on the shoulder would then turn to greet you. Subtle actions and nonverbal communication help bring robots to life. Envision a world with socially acceptable future robots with must-have attributes, such as artificial eyes that move and blink, slight chest movements that simulate breathing, and man-made muscles that change facial expressions.

Robin Hanson, author of _The Age of Em: Work, Love and Life When Robots Rule the Earth_, predicts that "We'll develop cheap technology for emulating brains on computers in the next 100 years."[13] Hanson's years of experience researching artificial intelligence lends to his expectation that emulations, or ems, will be similar to human brains but able to run one thousand times faster and be copied. Wow ... "uploaded brains" seem a little scary.

Please keep in mind that in Hanson's predictions in *The Age of Em* are looking one hundred years down the line. While these predictions are indeed possible, we assume that society will have protected itself against many of the dangers and risks of ems.

Think of the possibilities with a higher powered human brain. Pandemics could pop up and take the lives of millions of people in a moment, but with faster minds working on a solution, the cure could be found almost immediately. War could break out, and we could end up being the smartest dead people in history, but with more intelligence and less emotion, there is hope we will somehow eliminate the insanity of war. Climate change is threatening to devastate our world, but with cooperation between technology and humans, there is a belief that these issues can be solved.

Our society of robot friends will continue to expand and play an integral part in our world. I predict that we will have a society of robots in everything we do.

Impact of Robots on the Economy

It's difficult to talk about robots without a discussion about the effects on employment because the transition into robotic labor is already well on its way.

We are already seeing computers and machines making their way into the job market like we saw when Unimation created the first industrial robot, and it immediately began improving the production of General Motors Cars. It has affected jobs in agriculture as well, as human labor is rarely needed at all now with the development of tractors and other machines.

But this is just the beginning. The opportunities that robots present are relatively untapped. As they become more skilled and have more capabilities, many jobs that are currently occupied by humans will no longer be needed. Instead, those jobs will be replaced with robots that are more efficient, more productive, and cheaper.

If you were the owner of a company, and you had the opportunity to increase production at a significantly lower cost, would you take that opportunity? What if it meant letting go of a large part of your workforce? Unfortunately, in our economic world, we adapt or die, as market forces do not have the luxury of a conscience.

Robots are My Friends

19

Downside

Not all jobs will be in danger, but some of the ones that will be susceptible to being replaced by robots include jobs in <u>food service, accommodations, transportation, warehousing, and real estate</u>. Robots will threaten all jobs that can be easily duplicated. For instance, a robot can flip a burger, an autonomous car can drive from point a to point b, and a machine can shelve boxes.[14]

Unfortunately, we have already seen many blue-collar jobs impacted by technological advancements, and it isn't going to get any better. Eventually, blue-collar jobs may not exist for human beings at all. We will also start to see this trickle into white-collar work as well. It's uncertain to what extent, but it is only a matter of time.

Because we have never seen a time like this, it leaves us largely unprepared as a society. There is no educational system in place to educate our children and even adults for what we are about to experience. We don't know what will be needed and how we can provide value in an ever-changing world and it is hard to predict what our response will be to these major changes. Will we find a way to adapt? The fear is that many of us will be unequipped and therefore left behind. I am hoping to prepare you for what our future will bring and provide the edge you need.

Upside

Jobs that are safe for the meantime are those that include what is considered high-skill because the work contributed by the worker is rare and not easily replaceable. While robotic machines are better than humans at doing the same thing the exact same way over and over again, they are (at this point) significantly worse at using creativity, interacting socially, and thinking critically. When someone is good at a job that requires these cognitive skills, it's difficult for a machine to replicate the performance as well as a human being.

There will always be the need for humans in certain fields doing certain jobs. Historically, we as humans have always been able to adapt. Old industries do not die on their own. They die because a new industry is born through innovation and adaptation. Within a new industry, opportunities are born and jobs are created, and if the industry grows like it is expected, jobs become abundant. It's the cycle of economic disruption.

Morgan

❖

20

Think about television. When TV became the main form of entertainment, the radio industry naturally declined. But now think of all the different jobs in television and related to television entertainment. You have actors, singers, producers, directors, editors, writers, lights, sound, production, makeup artists, fashion designers, etc. Then you have TV spots and advertisers paying to run commercials on a network. Think about all the jobs on a TV network or in the advertising firm. There are too many jobs to count, and it all started because TV took over a large part of the market from radio.

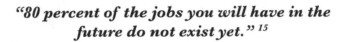

"80 percent of the jobs you will have in the future do not exist yet." [15]

—Mark Lautmanin, *When the Boomers Bail: A Community Economic Survival Guide*

Coexisting with Robots

The truth is, we don't even have the slightest clue how the increased role of robots will impact the job market. We know that there will be drastic changes, and we know some of the jobs that will no longer be an option, but to try to predict the new market and new positions that do not currently exist is like taking a shot in the dark.

One thing that can help us prepare for whatever is to come is to start by understanding the advantages of humans versus the advantages of robots. Erik Brynjolfsson, director of the Initiative on the Digital Economy for MIT, predicts in the January 2017 issue of the *McKinsey Global Institute Report* that the future of automation indicates that humans are better than robots at the following: spotting new patterns; logical reasoning; creativity; coordination between multiple agents; natural language understanding; identifying social and emotional states; responding to social and emotional states; displaying social and emotional states; and moving around diverse environments.[16] There are some things a robot simply cannot replicate, and this is where humans will continue to bring value.

We've already discussed in great detail the advantages of robots, but let's quickly recap. Robots offer quicker production with minimum errors and are able to work all hours of the day, every day of the week. Their work is very precise, and they are able to repeat their quality of work with great consistency. This gives them a productivity and efficiency that is unmatchable by human hands. This increased efficiency will have enormous effects on our world. The cost of everything from housing to food and from transportation to medical needs will decrease. Reduced costs will then lower the price of goods and services that will hopefully provide excess income to create personal affluence for our future lives. Yes, there is some optimism!

As technology advances, robots will continue to improve in areas like efficiency, speed, quality, and costs, and even the areas they currently struggle with, like critical thinking, creativity, and social interaction. This means that we, too, must continue to develop in the specific areas we already thrive. The skills we have that a robot cannot currently match, and may never be able to match, are where we add value.

In a separate report from the July 2016 issue of the *McKinsey Quarterly*, Michael Chui, James Manyika, and Mehdi Miremadi stated that analyzing work activities rather than occupations is a more accurate predictor of automation. Unpredictable physical work, stakeholder interactions, and applying expertise are less susceptible to automation. And managing others is least susceptible—so no robot bosses yet.[17]

We may not be sure the exact job title to strive for, or even the job description, but we do know we offer unique skills that robots do not have. So find your skills. Find what makes you unique. What makes you different? This is what will set you apart; then all that's left is figuring out how to utilize that skill in a way our world needs.

When you combine the skills of humans with the productivity and efficiency of robots, it's easy to see how we can coexist. In fact, the future looks even brighter. Robots will have a tremendous impact on our lives. The collaboration between humans and robots has

Morgan

22

been proven to be far more successful and productive than working separately. Robotics increase the accessibility to data centers all around the world, make us more efficient, and increase our financial viability. Robots are our friends.

Examples of Jobs in Robotic Technologies

Software Developer
Robotics Engineer
Robotics Service Technician

See more in Chapter 9, "Help Wanted"

Robots are My Friends

Medical Innovations

If you looked at the world we live in, with all its imperfections, and then could magically choose to fix one thing, what is the first thing you would change? Hatred? War? Social injustice? Poverty? Pollution? There are so many broken areas of our world that it's hard to choose just one thing to fix. However, if I could pick one I may decide to eliminate all diseases and health imperfections. By removing diseases, this could undoubtedly be the single most critical improvement to both the quality and longevity of our lives. And after all, that's really what technological advancements are meant to accomplish—improving the overall life for humanity for this generation and generations to come.

So maybe we don't have all the answers yet to eradicate diseases, but we are making massive headway by identifying, correctly diagnosing, and effectively treating all disease. The key to prevention and eventually elimination is early identification and preventative treatment. We've already seen massive medical advancements with improved technology, pharmaceutical advancements, the development of medical devices and equipment, but there is even more breakthrough coming in this field, and it's fascinating to explore some of the potential solutions in health care that are right around the corner.

Isaac Ro, a senior research analyst of life sciences at Goldman Sachs Research, believes that as advancements in the medical field continue to occur, we can expect to live longer lives.[18] It works in two ways: improved treatment and disease prevention.

Improved Treatment

Improvements in treatment are accomplished one step at a time. With better treatment, we can fight diseases and viruses more effectively. When we optimize the way we fight diseases, it will no longer be as devastating and threatening when a disease develops. It starts with improving the areas we have already established such as optimizing surgery using robots, enhancing pharmaceutical drugs with advanced research, further developing medical devices, and improving treatment products. These things are imminent with technological advancements.

Stem Cells

Technology has recently developed a very promising stem cell research program that is currently in the process of developing what Dr. Ronald P. Drucker considers the Superheroes of Healing. Stem cells are highly specialized cells that are formed in our bodies. Dr. Drucker explains "we rely on persisting stem cells to repair injured tissues and replace cells that are lost every day, such as those in our skin, hair, blood, muscles, nerves, lining of our gut, brain and all other the organs and glands."

Stem cells are truly remarkable. They are like a reserve our bodies have of replacement cells. Any cell that is damaged can simply be replaced by stem cells. The younger you are the more stem cells your body has to offer so as we age, our stem cells don't repair and regenerate cells, organs, and tissues as well as they once did.

Think of when you have a wound of some kind. It usually remains open for some time. However, you clean it up and cover the wound, and eventually, it will begin to close and heal itself. It used to be believed that when our bodies experience a cut through skin, fat, and muscle that over time the muscle and skin would grow into each other, ultimately closing the wound. This isn't the case! It's actually stem cells filling the cut and then transforming itself into the necessary skin, fat, and muscle needed to repair the wound.

Morgan

26

Stem cells have incredible regeneration powers. This is what allows them to transform themselves into any tissue-specific cell. Dr. Drucker states:

> This reparative power of stem cells has been identified as the key towards offering cell-based therapies to many chronic degenerative diseases such as; Congestive Heart Failure, Chronic Bronchitis, Emphysema, Asthma, C.O.P.D., Lupus, Rheumatoid Arthritis, Fibromyalgia, Crohn's Disease, Ulcerative Colitis, Parkinson's Disease, Multiple Sclerosis, ALS, Alzheimer's, Stroke, Cerebral Palsy, Degenerative Disk Disease, Diabetes, Diabetic Retinopathy, Diabetic Neuropathy, Macular Degeneration, Kidney Disease, Osteoarthritis, Erectile Dysfunction, and the entire host of Autoimmune Diseases.[19]

We are even beginning to see stem cells being utilized with injuries such as paralysis. So, while this is something that our body naturally possesses, we are just now learning new ways to use this weapon against diseases and injuries to improve and optimize our health. Regenerative medicine is trending toward becoming the future of medical treatment, and it's expected to revolutionize health care.

Our bodies are truly amazing! We have a miracle treatment within ourselves, and technology is finding ways to better utilize this amazing feature. We are just now fully unlocking it!

Liquid Biopsy

It's debatable, but out of every danger in the world, cancer often strikes the most fear in our hearts. Cancer is a group of diseases involving abnormal cell growth with the potential to invade or spread to other parts of the body. When it is caught early and has not spread throughout the body, it can be treated and cured. However, if caught in the later stages, oftentimes there is not a whole lot of treatment that can be done to remove the disease. Of course, there are always outliers, but the earlier cancer is found, the more success the treatment will have.

Screening tests like mammograms and colonoscopies have become a significant focus in the medical world to catch the early stages of cancer more often. We've seen cancers become much more treatable because of the success of these screening tests. New testing is continually being developed to catch more cancer forms at the earliest stage possible.

In an article titled *Liquid Biopsy*, Michael Standaert talks about this advanced technique of cancer testing developed by Dennis Lo. Lo is a doctor from Hong Kong who has spent twenty years developing "liquid biopsies." These are cancer screening tests that draw blood to detect the early stages of various forms of cancer, such as liver cancer. "That's possible because dying cancer cells also shed DNA into a person's blood." If cancer is in fact there, an annual blood test will catch it while it is still curable.

Not only would liquid biopsies help catch cancer at the very early stages but it could also potentially help doctors treat the type of cancer very specially. "Doctors can pick a drug according to the specific DNA mutation driving a cancer forward." If doctors can tell the exact mutation occurring in the body that is causing the cancer, they're able to use a more specialized treatment. If researches can clearly make the case that liquid biopsies save lives, Lo believes that this treatment will become mainstream.[20] I guess we will wait and see.

Nanotechnology

The most exciting treatment possibility that is still very much untapped is nanotechnology. I'll be honest, nanotechnology is an intimidating word. To hopefully make it less intimidating and more understandable let's break down the word. Nano means one billionth, and it is used in the formation of a compound word. For instance, a nanometer is the unit of measurement used in nanotechnology, and it is one billionth of a meter. For perspective, a sheet of paper is one hundred thousand nanometers thick. Therefore, nanotechnology is technology happening on a scale we have a hard time comprehending. Put more simply, Dr. Meskó Bertalan, known as the Medical Futurist explains, "Essentially, nanotechnology comprises science, engineering and technology conducted at the nanoscale, which is about 1 to 100 nanometers. It is basically manipulating and controlling materials at the atomic and molecular level."[21]

When we can shrink technology down to a scale this small, new opportunities become possible. Think about being able to attack disease as this level! It allows for highly targeted treatment which has many advantages.

Currently, our treatments cannot directly target the diseased tissue, so it is then forced to fight all tissues, healthy and unhealthy. While we obviously want to destroy the diseased tissue to rid of the overall disease, there is great risk and oftentimes brutal side effects that occur when the healthy tissue is also attacked. These side effects can often cause problems within the patient's body that is more damaging and sometimes even more dangerous than the original disease.

Chemotherapy provides an example of this. The chemo is sent into the body to kill all cancerous cells, so they stop reproducing and so the cancer stops spreading. But because of its lack of direct targeting, it cannot stop at only cancerous cells and kills other healthy ones as well. As I'm sure you know, this can cause many painful side effects that can be very dangerous.

However, with nanotechnology and its ability to attack disease at the micro level, it has the potential to be highly targeted when fighting illness in our bodies.

For instance, a real possibility is micro-sized robots that would swim through blood and other bodily fluids to deliver medical relief such as drugs in a highly-targeted way. Imagine sending intelligent robots small enough to navigate your body and destroy all diseased cells. Similar to the legendary video arcade game *Pac-Man*, traveling through your veins eating up and removing all the bad guys.

Another form of nanotechnology that is currently being developed is something called nanoswimmers. These are designed to swim through bodily fluids and deliver drugs that can directly target and fight disease tissue like cancer cells.[1]

While this sounds like a theory taken straight out of a science fiction novel, it is actually a growing and developing possibility.

When we know what a disease is and where and how it is attacking the body, a more targeted form of relief is going to be not only more effective but significantly safer as well. This would be revolutionary for cancer treatment. Nanotechnology opens the doors to our future medical world that were locked shut before.

Disease Prevention

The second way technological advancements will lengthen our lives is through disease prevention. While better treatment is greatly

Medical Innovations

important, preventing disease altogether removes any future need for treatment. If there is no illness or disease in the first place, there is no problem that needs fixing. Prevention should always be preferred to treatment.

Of course, it's not realistic to expect 100 percent prevention, but the first and most important goal is to find ways to prevent life-threatening illnesses.

Predicting Heart Disease

Heart disease is not a virus or bacteria, meaning that it cannot simply be cured once it is found. So, instead of sitting idly by and doing nothing, science is finding ways to predict heart attacks before they occur.

In the past, heart attacks have not been easily or accurately trackable even when monitoring weight and symptoms. This has caused science and medical research to be proactive in finding new methods for predicting heart failures.

John Boehmer, a cardiologist and professor of medicine at Penn State College of Medicine, has been studying whether the conditions of heart failure patients can be accurately tracked. Using advanced monitors and sensors, Dr. Boehmer and his team studied nine hundred heart failure patients. He found that the special regime of sensors spotted 70 percent of sudden heart attacks approximately thirty days before they occurred![22] This discovery can drastically impact the medical field and will greatly help in identifying heart attacks before they happen so they can hopefully be prevented.

With the medical advances of today and the increased awareness around heart disease, I believe that we will continue to see heart failures occurring later and later in life. We may never be able to get rid of them because aging is simply a part of life, but with improved research and a better understanding of how to take care of our bodies, we will be able to delay heart failures considerably.

DNA Modification

For as long as I can remember, genetic modification has always been a mysterious and highly intriguing potential advancement of the future. Much like flying cars, we've always been made to believe that it was indeed possible. However, the question was still when it would become a reality. Not just when but also the power behind it. Would it be able to fix any mutation? Would there be danger involved or error possibilities?

We've even seen it done in the past with plants, but the reason it has never advanced to humans is because of the randomness and lack of control. Scientists would zap plants with radiation to flip letters of DNA at random. They would shoot plant cells with various genes to alter the DNA codes. However, there was never any precision behind the actions, so it was never a possibility to advance into human genetics. Until now.

In 2012 scientists introduced Crispr (Clustered Regularly Interspaced Short Palindromic Repeats), a new and more precise DNA-editing technique. What makes Crispr so groundbreaking is its ability to make DNA editing cheap, easy, and precise. Only a few years after its introduction it has already been used to cure mice of HIV and hemophilia. That's just the beginning. Pig organs are being altered to make them suitable as human organ donors. A team at Harvard is looking to edit the DNA of modern-day elephants with the hope of resurrecting the wooly mammoth species. With the development that Crispr has seen in only a few short years, these dreams seem realistically possible.

Kyle Peterson, in an article from _The Wall Street Journal_, interviewed Jennifer Doudna, a Crispr pioneer. She explains how Crispr works. Essentially it is cutting out the mutated DNA, and then inserting a new, modified strand in its place.[23] To me, it sounds like copying and pasting in new DNA exactly where you want. It is so exact that's its nothing like we've ever seen!

However, when you are talking about altering genetics and DNA strands, there is risk involved, no matter how precise the procedure has proven to be. The human genome system contains 3.2 billion letters, and one simple error, unintended edit, or minor typo could result in complete disaster. But as advancements continue, and further research and experimentation is done, the risk will decrease, and the certainty of the procedure will increase.

There is an ethical argument that may never go away. Is it OK to edit the DNA of a human being? After all, that is what makes each of us unique. The thing that sets me apart from you. By editing our DNA, does that remove part of who we are?

Not only would Crispr be able to treat some of the diseases that have been uncurable up to this point but it also would potentially

Medical Innovations

31

be able to repair the DNA in our bodies that are responsible for the development of cancer. For example, the BRCA gene is a tumor suppressor, so when there is a mutation here, the body is less able to fight off tumors, increasing the likelihood of developing cancerous tumors. If we're able to fix this mutation, we're fighting cancer before it even forms.

Simply put, these medical advancement makes it increasingly likely that we will live longer and healthier lives. It means that living in good health without disabilities and well beyond one hundred years will be commonplace because of advancements in nanotechnology, stems cells, genetic modifications and liquid biopsy.

Our future is *now*, and we are all a part of its advancement. What if we could print a human heart? Science has found a way. That is precisely what is happening. Medicine is just the start, as nanotechnology and other advancements in medicine spill over throughout our entire world and transcend health care into every aspect of our world. Nanotechnology directly affects everything from medicine to manufacturing, from automotive to space, and from data storage to health.

Where will it all lead? I do not know, but when the medical field is working perfectly, diseases will be much more preventable, and those that do occur will be much more treatable. Ideal physical health is closer than many think.

Please keep in mind that while living longer and healthier lives seems like a dream come true, it does not guarantee an improved quality of life. Don't get me wrong—I believe that the medical advancements I have described will significantly benefit the world we live in and the individuals who live in it. But do not mistake physical health for the perfect life. You can have perfect physical health and still feel hurt or broken. Or you can be crippled by illness but still be filled with joy and happiness. Life is about so much more than what we often perceive as perfection. I believe the happiness you find in your life will come from purpose, passion, and love. Ideal physical health is simply the cherry on top!!

Morgan

Examples of Jobs in Medicine and Health Care

Stem Cell Researcher
Genetics Counsellor
Nanotechnology Engineer

See more in Chapter 9, "Help Wanted"

The Future of Transportation

ichael Ronen, head of Investment Banking at Goldman Sachs, stated, "The automotive industry is undergoing a profound change that will completely reimagine mobility. The transformation of cars into electric and fully autonomous vehicles in the coming years, combined with the business model shift from car ownership to utilizing the shared economy will upend the auto industry, with implications for the finance, insurance and real estate sectors."

The automobile industry has benefited greatly from technological advancements, and we are still only in the very early stages of artificial intelligence-controlled autonomous vehicles (AVs). These advancements are sure to change automobile history and even the course of humanity.

Electrical Energy

We have already seen cars begin to shift to electric energy. The primary fuel source in the past has been gasoline, much to the objection from environmentalists and conservationists. Bob Koort, head of Industrials and Materials research for Goldman Sachs Research, refers to lithium as <u>the newer and better gasoline</u>. Because of its abundance and low density, lithium is the ideal metal to use for rechargeable batteries. Its energy density allows for the battery to store enough energy to have a powerful car without the need to recharge the battery frequently.

Bob Koort predicts that by the year 2025, electric vehicles will make up 22 percent of the automotive market, up from the 3 percent it currently occupies. For every 1 percent increase in market share, Goldman Sachs Research expects lithium demand to rise 70,000 tons per year. With the current lithium market producing just 160,000 tons annually, demand for electric vehicles alone could triple the size of the entire lithium market by 2025.[24]

Automakers like Tesla Motors must continue to make progress in lithium technology if they hope to match the growth and saturation of their forebears at the turn of the twenty-first century. There have already been significant advancements in the production of lithium-ion battery packs, which has caused the price of electric vehicles to drop. As improvements continue, we will see electric vehicles becoming more cost friendly and new opportunities becoming available.

Even with the recent growth of electric vehicles, they still only hold a small share of the transportation market. There are still many new possibilities. As development continues one area being explored is batteries for large vehicles such as heavy trucks, trains, and airplanes. Tapping into this new market would create additional lithium demand sources.[25]

Autonomous Vehicles

Autonomous vehicles require a technology platform that includes GPS navigation, chips, sensors, radar, cameras, and software. These AVs need to be able to take all that data coming from inside and outside the vehicle and use it to make smart decisions in real time.

In 2015 an Audi SQ5 drove thirty-four hundred miles across the country almost completely "hands-free" without the assistance of a human driver. The car guided itself from San Francisco to New York through big-city traffic, road construction, confusing street signs, and diverse weather conditions. Throw in careless human drivers, and you are really putting AV tech through its paces. Minus two moments when a human driver had to step in, the rest of the trip was a leisurely experience for the one behind the wheel.

After the trip was completed, a few quick software fixes were made with the goal of making the next cross-country trek truly 100 percent hands-free.

Another example of the driverless revolution taking shape is in the mining industry. According to Sam Tracy of the *Huffington Post* points out that large trucks are being used to haul ore out of the mines to be refined and processed nearby. Rio Tinto, a multinational mining company, has completely automated its trucks at a site in Australia. Canadian oil company Suncor Energy shortly followed suit. These trucks drive very slowly on a fixed route that does not include any public roads making this operation possible.[26] Even with these regulations, this is still a significant step forward in the auto industry, and we will continue to feel the ripple effects. The self-driving car of tomorrow is quickly on its way.

Zack Kanter, Entrepreneur and guest contributor for CBS San Francisco Bay Area News states that both Google and Tesla predict that by 2020 we will see fully autonomous cars on the road. Fully autonomous simply means the car is 100 percent self-reliant, and the person in the car is not needed one bit. They could go to sleep and wake up at their destination.[27]

With 1.2 million fatal car accidents every year, there is a lot of danger currently involved in driving. Self-driving cars have the potential to improve transportation safety and significantly reduce this danger on the roads. Automobile accidents occur every sixty thousand miles or so, but with autonomous driving, that rate drops to one accident every six million miles. If every car on the road was self-driving, approximately a million lives would be saved each year. With a tangible number as significant as that, it shouldn't even be a question to further explore the advancements and possibilities of autonomous vehicles. We may never have a 100 percent safe and error-free transportation system, but the question remains: What is the safest option? So are autonomous vehicles safer than human drivers? The answer is very clear: yes!

Effects of Autonomous Vehicles

The shift to increased AV availability will have a profound impact on several markets. Sam Tracy of the *Huffington Post*, also indicates that once the AV movement starts to become more mainstream, it will revolutionize the transportation industry and replace millions of jobs, from taxi drivers to truckers. Automotive companies will be challenged to keep up with the driverless trend, along with all businesses associated with car sales, auto repair services, parts manufacturers, oil companies, and insurance sectors.

For example, with autonomous vehicles offering safer travel, the car insurance industry is beginning to look much less stable. There has always been a great demand and need for auto insurance because of the likelihood of accidents. But as autonomous vehicles begin to take control of the market, and the technology involved in AV gets better, accidents will become less and less likely. With accidents becoming nearly nonexistent, car insurance may no longer be a necessity. Rates will plummet, bringing financial instability to insurance companies.

I know economic disruption can be alarming, but fortunately, this is not projected to happen overnight. The driverless movement is certainly happening, but at a cautious pace because of its challenges and risks. Our political system, which typically is not a fan of change, is slowing down the development process as maybe they should, but it can't stop the train of progress forever.

Regardless, change is happening, and the disruptive innovation of autonomous vehicles is projected to be massive.

Kanter believes that autonomous vehicles will remove almost all need for consumers to own cars. With cars being such an expensive investment, ride-sharing services like Uber are already more economical than owning a car if you live in a city and drive less than ten thousand miles per year. To fully understand Kanter's prediction, we have to look to the future. Factor in that autonomous vehicles would remove any need for the driver of the rideshare service, which for a company like Uber, make 75 percent of the transportation fare. With autonomous vehicles, this expense becomes non-existent, and ridesharing becomes even more economical for the rider. Also influencing this movement is the expected growth of urban life and the population in cities. According to a study by the United Nations, approximately 82 percent of the US population lives in urban areas, and that number is expected to approach 90 percent by 2050. This only further enhances the idea that owning a car will be unnecessary as public transportation and ridesharing options are simplified in big cities.[28]

The potential here is that it could become cheaper for most everyone to use a ride-sharing service than own a vehicle. Essentially, this removes the need to own a car for people like us. Ride-sharing and car-sharing companies will become the ones who are primarily buying cars.

The disruption doesn't stop here. In the 2015 article *How Uber's Autonomous Cars Will Destroy 10 Million Jobs And Reshape The Economy By 2025*, Kanter states:

> Disruptive innovation does not take kindly to entrenched competitors – like Blockbuster, Barnes and Noble, Polaroid, and dozens more like them; it is unlikely that major automakers like General Motors, Ford, and Toyota will survive the leap. They are geared to produce millions of cars in dozens of different varieties to cater to individual taste and have far too much overhead to sustain such a dramatic decrease in sales. I think that most will be bankrupt by 2030, while startup automakers like Tesla will thrive on a smaller number of fleet sales to operators like Uber by offering standardized models with fewer options.

Massive automakers have owned the industry for so long, but with such revolutionary innovations, it's hard to believe they will be able to last.

You can also say goodbye to professional drivers. Along with Uber, Lyft, and taxi drivers, the delivery industry will also be affected. There are fourteen million driver-related employees in the US, including long-haul truckers, local delivery drivers, forklift operators, bus drives, and food delivery drivers. As autonomous vehicles are perfected, all these positions will no longer be occupied by humans. Not only will this be safer but much more cost efficient.

Feeling discouraged yet? Don't be! I want to remind you that time and time again we have seen innovation create massive new job opportunities in their growing and evolving industry. It's hard to know exactly what kind of career opportunities will become available, but keep your mind open because there are sure to be some awesome ones!

The Future of Transportation

Futuristic Transportation in the Making

Flying Cars

Flying cars have been a dream of ours since the invention of airplanes. They became popularized by futuristic entertainment such as *The Jetsons* back in the sixties and *Back to the Future*'s DeLorean DMC-12 in the eighties. Many talented dreamers have attempted but failed to make the flying car a reality. A car that doubles as an airplane operates in different physics, and engineering environments pose challenges, along with consideration of aviation rules, guidelines, and management.

Despite all that, the dream of the flying car is very much still alive. Over the past ten years, scores of start-up companies have proposed a new generation of dual-purpose vehicles. Private investors hoping to develop the flying car exist throughout the industry, and some have successfully developed models that have addressed and overcome many obstacles. Some of the most encouraging creations are being developed by Terrafugia Corporation, a private sector company with a mission to design a feasible, attractive flying car. Additionally, the Pentagon's Defense Advanced Research Projects Agency (DARPA) funded millions to build a flying Humvee vehicle, and NASA is designing a one-person electric helicopter/aircraft hybrid for commuters. These are encouraging signs that this is just another challenge that technology *will* conquer.

Space Travel

In January 1986, the <u>*Challenger* space shuttle</u> (OV-99) exploded only seventy-three seconds into its launch, killing all seven of its crew members.[29] This devastation caused the space industry to stagnate for years; however, it is beginning to make headway, and space is again a topic of discussion and intrigue. "Space is becoming smaller, closer, and cheaper, reinventing an industry that has stagnated for decades and making room for new applications, new technologies, and competitors," says <u>Noah Poponak</u> in an article by PR Newswire.[30]

China is developing a hypersonic plane. In <u>*A Look at China's Most Exciting Hypersonic Aerospace Programs*</u>, Jeffrey Lin and P. W. Singer explain this plan "can fly in the 'near-space' altitude of 12 miles to 60 miles, allowing it to shoot into orbit with integrated rockets, or fly civilian and military missions in near space."[31] The innovation of this hypersonic aircraft is expected to boost China to the forefront of the aerospace industry.

The China Aerospace Science and Technology Corporation (CASC) is mining the best talent and technology in the aerospace field to create the next generation of hybrid planes and spacecraft. The space plane will be able to take off from an airport landing strip and blast into orbit because of its combined cycle engine.

Hyperloop Trains

Fox News recently reported on the development of the hyperloop train, named SpaceX, another, Elon Musk creation that is sure to transform train transportation. "Rising on nearly airless tubes at 800 mph, the train will transport you from LA to San Francisco in just 30 minutes."[32]

Transportation is continually changing with new technological advancements. It's unclear what will and won't happen in the next several years and even the next few decades. However, what is clear is that there is a hunger for innovation in this industry. There will continue to be searching for new and better innovative developments that will open up new job opportunities. The industry will create plenty of new jobs, and this will require a tremendous amount of talent and bright and creative minds.

Examples of Jobs in Transportation

Drones Engineer
Autonomous Vehicles Programmer
Clean Car Engineer

See more in Chapter 9, "Help Wanted"

The Future of Transportation

Departments of Energy

A t this point, most everyone is aware of the energy crisis we are experiencing. It's a complex issue that we are attempting to solve utilizing our advanced technology.

To briefly explain the issues behind the crisis, fossil fuel has dominated the energy market for the past two hundred years and is used to produce electricity, or it is refined to use as fuel for heating and transportation. To put it simply, the world runs on fossil fuel.[33]

Oil, coal, and natural gas are all examples of fossil fuel. Part of the issue is that at the current rate at which we are using fossil fuels our world will enter into an energy shortage before the end of the century. And since fossil fuel is formed naturally from prehistoric plants and animals being buried by layers of rock, and it is nonrenewable, we are unable to create more. Once we run out, there's no way to access more, and it will eventually run out.

The other part of the crisis deals with the preservation and condition of the world we live in. Not the societal world but the physical world, as in planet Earth.

Fossil fuel goes through a process to create energy that includes burning it. When it is burned, it produces a large amount of greenhouse gases, such as carbon dioxide and methane. For this reason, it is considered a dirty source of energy. Clean energy, on the other hand, produces very little—if any—greenhouse gases.

Greenhouse gases cause the earth's atmosphere to warm, which causes the climate change we hear so much about in the news and media. We already see some of the effects of global warming, and many scientists believe that as more greenhouse gases are produced, the consequences will become even more drastic. The weather will become more extreme, the spread of disease will increase, and the world we live in will be threatened.[34]

So, while it seems like a bad thing that fossil fuel energy is disappearing, to me it appears to be a blessing in disguise. It is leading many companies in the energy industry to explore alternative and clean energy sources—just what the earth needs. Not only would these alternative energy sources be clean but they would also be renewable, meaning we can use the energy repeatedly. This would not only solve the energy supply shortage, but also would provide environmentally friendly energy that preserves the world we live in so future generations can enjoy our beautiful world.

While the development of renewable clean energy sources has been somewhat slow up to this point, it is expected it to start progressing rather quickly because the issue is becoming critical to our health, our economy, and our future.

With an increased focus on producing clean and renewable energy, I believe this could spark a battery boom. We will need to find ways to store the energy created to fulfill its true potential, and batteries could play a vital role in this objective. Manufacturers are already rushing to fill the vacuum. Mercedes-Benz has pulled the wraps off its first home energy storage kits. In 2015 Tesla Motors underwent development for a similar Powerwall product.

Thanks to large-scale factory investments by Tesla Motors, LG Chem Michigan Inc., and others, battery costs have plummeted 80 percent in six years. The lower prices created by these advancements mean that more energy will be available, and more industries and customers can use them cost-effectively.

It's not easy to predict the energy sources that will replace fossil fuel. After all, it's dominated the world's energy market for over two hundred years. But there are an array of options and new forms of energy that are in development as you read this, and I want to explore a few of the various options that our world could eventually lean on.

Solar Energy

Solar energy is the process of harnessing the energy from the sun. Considering the sun is our greatest source of energy, solar energy has the potential to be the most abundant source of power on Earth. Currently, the solar industry is growing at 30 percent a year; and while solar is only 1 percent of US energy consumption today, if we can keep up that compounding effort, it could be our primary source of energy in fifteen to twenty years. The potential is there.

We are still learning new and more effective ways to capture and convert this energy for our benefit. The energy is there for the taking, but technology will need to advance for us to harness this solar energy efficiently. One idea includes turning every window into a solar panel. This would allow windows and glass sheets to harvest the energy from light that the naked eye cannot see.

In the past, this was inconceivable because of the cost of solar panels. With limited research, the cost to produce solar energy was very high and unaffordable for families and many businesses. But with the growth we have seen recently, the cost of gathering solar energy has dropped drastically. This is making it increasingly possible for solar energy to become an affordable solution for homeowners and businesses.[35]

Wind Power

Wind power is simply harnessing the energy that wind creates. Humans have been using wind as a source of power for thousands of years. It was originally used to crush grain and pump water, but recently we have seen development to utilize the power of wind in other forms, such as creating electricity. They now stand about 270 feet high with 170-foot blades. One of the largest and fastest-growing wind markets in the world is in the United States. With advancements continuing in this technology, the wind market will create new job opportunities and boost overall economic growth.

Even though wind is one of the oldest forms of energy, we are only beginning to scratch the surface of its potential. There is so much more that wind can do for us if we only find new ways to control it. We have seen wind turbines increase in size and height

Departments of Energy

because higher altitudes produce higher winds.[36] Since higher wind speeds produce greater electricity, taller turbines capture more wind power. There has also been a development of the first offshore wind farm because of higher winds at sea. There have also been ideas to create <u>autonomous and flying wind farms</u> to thrive where winds are strongest.[37]

As production and technology continue to improve, we will find better ways to harness the power of wind. The wind industry will play a huge role in the energy strategy to cut greenhouse gases and dirty sources of energy. It will continue to diversify the already developing energy economy and market.

Water Energy

Water energy, or <u>hydropower</u>, uses the flow of water to produce electricity. Dams and other water powering facilities allow us to control and harness the energy that water stores.

About 7 percent of US electricity is generated from hydropower, making it the largest renewable source of energy out there. But again, much like with other forms of renewable and clean energy, this market is mostly untapped. Before now, there has not been a substantial need or sense of urgency to explore the potentials of hydropower.

There are currently eighty thousand dams in the US, but only 3 percent of those dams are used to produce power.[38] These dams are already built, meaning there is an excellent opportunity to further utilize many of these dams for energy purposes.

While hydropower is already very much developed, <u>marine and hydrokinetics</u> represent an emerging industry that is still being explored. This technology converts the energy from waves, tides, and currents into electricity. With 70 percent of the world covered in water, and ocean tides and currents flowing naturally, there is enormous untapped potential in the energy produced by moving water. There is enough energy only along the US coastlines to meet a large portion of the country's power needs.

An example of harnessing the ocean's power is through a buoy. As the buoy sits in the ocean and moves back and forth and up and down due to the current, it can store the energy created by the movement. One of the challenges scientists and engineers face is producing devices that can withstand the harsh conditions created by the powerful flow of water.[39]

There is still much more that wave, tidal, and hydropower can produce. It will take critical research and development to expand water-powered electricity generation. With the development of new technologies, water energy will become more efficient in making the production capacity greater. Water energy will play a significant role in powering homes and businesses in the US for years to come.

Nuclear Power

Nuclear power uses nuclear fission, or the splitting of uranium atoms, to generate energy. We have used nuclear power for the past sixty years, and it currently contributes 20 percent of the electricity generated in the US. This consists of 56 percent of the of America's clean energy.[40] Since nuclear power produces low-carbon energy, it is safe and non-threatening to our world.

Much like the other forms of clean energy that I have mentioned, nuclear power still has much more it can potentially offer with technological advancements. Scientists and engineers are continually looking for ways to improve nuclear reactors. According to Wikipedia, "A nuclear reactor, formerly known as an atomic pile, is a device used to initiate and control a self-sustained nuclear chain reaction."[41]

For example, small modular reactors are being developed where they would be able to be transported to sites, and ready to go upon arrival. This would reduce cost and construction times. Engineers are also looking to extend the operating lifetime of current plants beyond sixty years by improving production.[42] Small but massive technological advancements in the nuclear power field can pay considerable dividends in costs, production, safety, and efficiency. There will always be new improvements that can be made—not just in this field but essentially everything.

Solar energy, wind power, water energy, and nuclear power are not the only sources of energy that will play a large role in our world's future. I believe each and every one of these four sources of energy will have a significant impact on our future, but many other sources are still being developed and even discovered. Renewable and clean energy will soon power the world, and it won't be a one-person show.

The pattern we've seen throughout history is that when new technology is developed, old technology dies, even if we aren't ready for it. This typically alters and disrupts an entire job market. But the interesting thing about change is that when an innovation is introduced, it generally replaces the old and brings in the new. With this change, some jobs will die, but new jobs will be created. Yes, fossil fuel–produced energy will soon be dead, as well as the jobs associated with the field. But with its death, there is an opportunity for the renewable energy industry to flourish.

As the renewable energy field grows and develops, new jobs will form. So, while I discussed the direction energy is heading at length, the purpose was not only to inform you of the latest technology in development or the climate change we are working to prevent. The goal is for you to see where the industry is headed to understand how you can potentially thrive in this field.

Does developing renewable energy interest you? Do you have a passion for preserving the earth? Are you interested in finding new, safer forms of energy to benefit our world?

The question you should always ask yourself is, "Is this an industry that I would enjoy?" Even if you don't know exactly how you fit in, it's the perfect starting place. Because if you find a field or area that you enjoy, you will find a way to offer value and make an impact in that field.

Examples of Jobs in Energy

Renewable Energy Researcher
Environmental Scientist
Hydropower Strategy Director

See more in Chapter 9, "Help Wanted"

Education for Tomorrow

Education opens the door to opportunities and experiences that have the power to change your world. It teaches you how to think and how to access your imagination and creativity. It is the basis for all the knowledge you will obtain over the course of your life. If you want to live a successful life and make some money while you're at it, this chapter, together with chapter 9 (Help Wanted), could be the most important twenty pages you will ever read. Ok, maybe that is a little overstated. But then, perhaps not!

"The more you learn, the more you earn."

— Frank A. Clark, author and poet

I write this chapter with mixed emotions, as on the one hand, our educational system is the most incredible source of brain power the world has ever seen. It provides our young and talented individuals the opportunity to study in an educational environment while at the same time providing social and emotional growth that is equally important to their journey. On the other hand, however, *The World Economic Forum*, together with the rest of the world indicates that

75% of the universities will be out of business in the next twenty-five years. Please understand, while this may have some merit, the university system is rapidly changing and adjusting to this potential scenario. Additionally, please realize they are talking twenty-five years from now.

The curriculum and areas of study available to college students incorporate the appropriate credentials your future employers will be seeking. Additionally, the collection of intellectual talent and infusion of knowledge is everywhere creating an electrifying environment. This, combined with thirty thousand young and talented individuals with a healthy social life, are attempting to find their professional niche while expanding future value.

The majority of jobs offering the highest salaries are those that deal with the Science, Technology, Engineering and Math (STEM). Conventional wisdom states that the income we earn is tied directly to the education we receive. Therefore, securing a college degree in any of these disciplines is a wise decision, as it will potentially provide you with a higher salary and more employment opportunity.

"The object of education is to prepare the young to educate themselves throughout their lives."

— Robert Hutchins, philosopher; chancellor and president, University of Chicago

We often think of education as the time spent in school and classes. While school is a formal version of education, it is not the only way to gain knowledge. We often neglect to include the education we receive progressing through life. The ability to reason logically, our cognitive thinking, our mental conceptualization ability and even the ability to multitask are all examples that are not necessarily learned in the classroom.

In *Learning by Doing: The Real Connection between Innovation, Wages, and Wealth*, author and economist James Bessen states, "You have to get rid of the idea that we go to school once when we're young, and that covers us for our entire career."[43] Our teachers, mentors, and coaches teach us how to think; our likes and interests teach us what to think about; and our preparation and experience teach us how to apply what we think to what we do. Formal education is essential but just the start. You now need to use these educational disciplines in the rapidly evolving world.

Peter Smith, a writer for the Baltimore Sun, in his article *Recognize Value of Experience, (June 24, 2018)* explains how our educational system is changing. The institutions of higher learning with the advent of the GI Bill, the affluence of the American workers, the community college movement and the advancements in technology have changed the face of the world as it pertains to our higher education and employment. Education, together with the increasing value of experience, has played a significant role in realigning the pathway to jobs.

The point of education is not necessarily to gain remarkable intelligence or have a plethora of facts and statistics on hand at all times, as our computers can provide that. The real purpose of education is to expand your mind to think and solve problems. With an improved and expanded mind, you can respond to challenges with greater awareness and understanding, which enables you to increase your knowledge and value.

I am a firm believer that the reason education is important is to develop the skills needed to solve problems. That includes forming a plan, working through issues or problems, following instructions, channeling your focus and critical thinking. Formal education provides a way to challenge and grow our minds and to prepare us for our futures.

Education is achieved in many ways. Life is full of educational opportunities to learn, and you will help yourself a great deal by taking advantage of those opportunities when they present themselves. I played football for Michigan State University. It's a common perception that the skills learned from athletics or music or art don't translate to the real world, but that is a misconception. There are many skills I developed thru the participation in athletics that directly translate into my everyday life. Hard work, dedication, teamwork and establishing a game plan are some of life's lessons you can't learn in your math class. While I do not want to downplay the value of formal education, I believe that education and knowledge can be achieved in many ways.

Broken Educational System

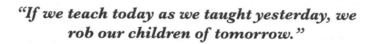

"*If we teach today as we taught yesterday, we rob our children of tomorrow.*"

—John Dewey, philosopher, psychologist, and education researcher

The Problem with Our Current System

If I were to ask every single teenager in the United States what they want to do when they grow up, I believe that most would not have an answer. And that's OK. Not only is it OK, but it's completely normal. With the current model for education, we're forcing our students to make important decisions regarding the rest of their lives that, frankly, we have never prepared them to make.

Many assume they are supposed to attend a college immediately following high school graduation, not because they have their life plan figured out but simply because that is what we tell them they need to do to succeed. While a college education *can* lead to a bright future, it is not the *only* formula that creates success. So a college education may be the best option for some, but it's certainly not the only option for everyone.

One of my concerns with our current educational system is the financial cost associated with a college degree. Students are graduating from college with a bachelor's degree and $100,000 or more in student loan debt. And worse yet they still have an unclear vision of what their career aspirations look like.

We are seeing high school graduates attending college with no career direction. It's one thing to attend college with specific plans and aspirations that require a higher education, but to send students off to college with no idea of what they want to do seems like a mistake. Too many students are graduating from college with a generic degree, a ton of student loan debt, no real-world experience, and not a clue what they want to pursue as a career. So a common pattern is to then pursue a master's degree.

Unfortunately, it's not always done to further their education and become more prepared for the job of their dreams, but instead to prolong the process of figuring out what to do with their life. It puts a hold on paying off student loans and allows students a couple more years to figure out their life plan, but it doesn't provide a solution. Instead, it amounts to higher student debt and takes away the opportunity to develop real-world skills and advance their resume. Again, a master's degree can be extremely valuable to some, but it is not for everyone.

The current educational system is broken and in danger of a complete meltdown unless it changes. The world has changed, and the job market has changed. The educational system in place is proving to be unsustainable, and change is needed for it to offer students real worth again.

Jessica Hullinger, in the 2015 article titled _This Is the Future of College_, wrote "It's not the death of higher education, but college as we've known it will be forced to undergo some dramatic changes in the next decade." She continued to state, "For years, college was the best pathway of finding a job. But as costs continue to rise and the percentage of graduates finding work falls, students are beginning to wonder: What's the real value of a college education?" Students are being charged a ridiculous amount of money that will take years, sometimes even decades, to pay off for skills that sometimes can be learned from an apprenticeship, internship or an online course.

Not only is a college education losing its value because of its extreme cost but it no longer provides students the proper preparation for what employers are looking for and what job openings require. According to a survey from St. Louis Community College, 60 percent of employers believe job applicants lack the necessary interpersonal and communication skills that they need. Hullinger states, "They can pass a calculus exam, but they can't identify or solve problems on the job, or negotiate, or lead a meeting." And Michael F. Maciekowich, the national director of HR consulting firm Astron Solutions LLC, states "In our business, there's a competency required that is not learned in school."[44] College is no longer opening the door to employment opportunities that it once did. It no longer sets a candidate apart and often leaves an employer looking for more. Now internships, apprenticeships, and real-life experience are needed on top of a college education to open up employment opportunities.

I hope it is becoming clear to you that for what a college education offers, it is not always worth its current cost. If you're at the point where you are contemplating pursuing a bachelor's or master's degree, ask yourself some hard questions. How much will it cost you? Can you obtain financial support and scholarships? What will it provide you? Is it needed for your career aspirations? Will it prepare you for your future? What else is required on top of the degree to obtain your dream job? And, oh, by the way, have you spent the time researching and attempting to determine what that dream job is?

The Change That is Needed

Google's top-rated Futurist Speaker, Thomas Frey, predicts severe danger for the future of America's colleges and universities. In his article titled, _The Future of Colleges & Universities_, he states, "Learning will become separated from the classroom. Courses will be created organically and formed around an on-demand, any-time, any-place delivery models. Professors will declare their independence and work for multiple institutions rather than just one specific college. Accreditation will shift from the Institution to the course and the individual. And textbooks, the ink-on-paper version that we know today, will all but disappear."[45] In most cases, colleges will price themselves right out of business.

It is entirely possible that within the next ten to fifteen years, the college experience will become rapidly unbundled. Lecture halls will disappear, the role of the professor will transform, and advancing technology will help make a college education much more attainable and valuable than it has been. Online classes are growing in popularity, and they will only become even more common and economical. The work office, where in some cases, more is learned in a few months than in an entire year at a university, may become the new classroom.

Paid apprenticeships could replace undergraduate education, and we are already starting to see this movement take place. Large corporations such as Amazon, JPMorgan Chase & Co., and Accenture PLC are discussing paid apprenticeships as a viable option. It would allow for specialized on-the-job technical training that supplements educational support. For example, Amazon is partnering with local community colleges to train current hourly workers into tech jobs within the company. If this system finds success, it will likely become an increasingly popular option among high school grads. This is just one of the many changes we are likely to see in the future of education.

These ensuing changes will likely cause many academic institutions and universities to shut down, but those that survive will be more innovative, efficient, and focus on developing skills rather than simply fulfilling a specific number of credit hours. Employers will spend more time and resources educating and recruiting their workforce. And employees who have long looked for benefits like vacation time and insurance options will soon value companies that provide education and training. Our world is rapidly changing, and our educational system needs to change with it so it can better prepare students for the life that lies ahead.

Finding Your Passions

"It is better to know some of the questions than all of the answers."

—James Thurber, author and humorist

Education and occupation are dependent upon one another. As we look into the future with the purpose of solidifying the direction we choose for ourselves, it becomes increasingly important to evaluate our possibilities. If you want to be an engineer but don't like math, it might not work out. If you don't enjoy science, then I probably wouldn't recommend becoming a doctor. The right career for you will challenge you to work within your strengths and passions.

Instead of asking, "What do you want to do when you grow up?" we should be asking things like, "What do you like to do?"; "What are you good at?"; "What are your interests and passions?"; and "What problem do you see in the world that you would like to fix?" It doesn't matter if you're sixteen or sixty, never stop asking yourself the hard questions that will help you better understand yourself. As you go through life, you will continue to learn new things about yourself. You will discover new skills you never knew you had. You will find new passions that capture your heart. You will find new purposes for your life.

I call these inner discussions of the mind, "meetings with yourself." The ability to know the right questions to ask of yourself will assist you in determining where it is that you want to go. Spend some time every week, or even every day, to crawl inside your head and ask yourself the tough questions that teach you about yourself. Force yourself to examine every part of you. Your motives, your passions, your loves, your values and what's important to you. We often assume we already have everything figured out, but we don't. Life moves so quickly that if you don't take the time to specifically examine yourself, you won't ever know who you really are. As you find your true identity, the rest of your life will begin to take shape.

Aptitude Testing

Aptitude tests can help you find your greatest skills and strengths. They also help you identify who you are and better understand why you are the way that you are. This can help you position yourself to live a life that allows you to succeed. They can provide value to most everyone, but primarily they're suited for those facing a major decision in life. For this reason, they are great for those choosing a major, choosing a career, or making a career switch.

These tests ask simple questions that require some inner digging to help people identify who they are. Using a highly intelligent algorithm, helpful insights are generated using the final results from the questions answered to lead the test taker in the right direction. Here are just a few of the many professional organizations that I highly recommend for interest and aptitude testing.

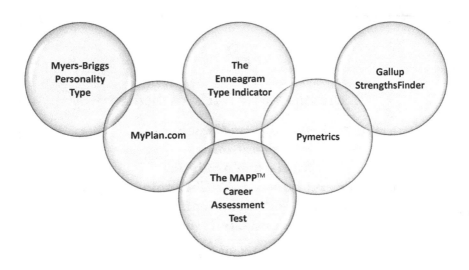

The tests are fun and can help you better understand yourself. It allows you to examine yourself to learn how you think, the way your brain analyzes thoughts, and helps identify your areas of strengths and aptitudes. What I personally love about these tests is that there are no right or wrong answers. You always get an A.

These tests don't plan out your entire life. They don't tell you exactly what career to pursue or what to choose as a major. They simply provide you recommendations to get you started on the right foot. It's a process, and changes along the way are ok and expected.

Don't allow yourself to be pressured by these tests or anyone else. The tests can get it wrong, your parents can give bad advice, and your teachers can lead you down the wrong path. Only you know what is best for you because this is *your* life, and these are *your* decisions. But with that in mind, life is not a solo sport. The people around you and the resources provided to you should help you find your true self and encourage you to do the things you are scared to do. They should never decide your life for you, but they should help steer you in the right direction. Your choices don't have to be permanent, your career selection can be temporary, and the road you choose does not have to lead to your final destination.

Examples of Fields of Study

Accounting/Finance
Economics
Statistics/Analytics
Computer and Information Technology/Science
Mechanical and Electrical Engineering
Computer and Civil Engineering

See more in Chapter 9, "Help Wanted"

Chapter

Help Wanted

believe this is the most crucial chapter in this book. It will outline the direction of education and the job market. It will layout potential promising opportunities while taking into account the technology-driven world we are experiencing and how rapidly its innovations are accelerating. My problem in attempting to identify and recommend future jobs and professions is that the majority of them have not been identified yet. At this point, you should clearly be able to see that technology, engineering, medical science, robotics, anything computers, energy and energy storage will have a massive impact on our world and economy. However, it's difficult to predict what the new products will be or what the specific opportunities will look like—just that they will most likely involve knowledge in the basic science, technology, engineering, and math fields. Our world is rapidly changing, and so is the job market.

Stephen Hawking, the accomplished physicist, once stated, "The automation of factories has already decimated jobs in traditional manufacturing, and the rise of artificial intelligence is likely to extend this job destruction deep into the middle class with only the most caring, creative or supervisory roles remaining." Hawking's vision, while a little intimidating, isn't far from becoming a reality. Specific industries and positions were once thought to be immune from such threats, but we now realize all fields and positions will be affected.

While it seems devastating for the future job market, this pattern has happened throughout history. Innovative disruption is not new. For example, 41 percent of American workers in 1900 were employed in the agriculture industry. By 2000 automated machinery reduced that number down to just 2 percent. But just because the agricultural industry no longer employs a large number of people, doesn't mean our economy is suffering.

When automation came to the textile industry, the price of clothes drastically dropped, which in turn created more demand for clothes and thus the need to increase more workers to operate and maintain the automated systems.

ATMs were thought to be the death of bank tellers. At first, the number of bank tellers per bank did drop; however, ATMs reduced the cost to operate banks and enabled them to increase the number of branches. Therefore, the need for tellers and other bank employees actually increased. You see, we learn to adapt, and we will continue to do that even during the boom in technology. Advancements will destroy jobs, but they also create new and often better opportunities.

My task here is to help you see the potential careers of the future and how you can attain knowledge in those areas so you can start moving in the right direction. Change is difficult, and it presents a lot of challenges. There is no doubt that many will struggle to find their place in our world that will soon be run by technology. I believe that earlier generations (pre-Generation X) may have a hard time adapting, especially if they have been in the same industry using the same skill set for years. There is some truth behind the saying "you can't teach an old dog new tricks." My hope with this book is to prepare for change *now*. There is hope for you!

Promising Fields of Study

STEM is an acronym used worldwide that stands for science, technology, engineering, and mathematics. STEM is typically used when addressing education policy and curriculum choices in school systems to improve and encourage competitiveness in science and technology developments. This is truly the gold standard for the educational expertise that is required for the technological advancements of today and tomorrow.

Morgan

The United States has developed into a global technological leader, in large part, through the genius and hard work of its scientists, engineers, and innovators, whether homegrown in the US or imported. Our world is becoming increasingly complex, where success is driven not only by *what* you know but by what *do* with what you know. It's more important than ever for you to be equipped not only with the knowledge learned by studying the areas of science, technology, engineering, and math, but equally important is the skills to solve tough problems, like gathering and evaluating evidence, and the ability to communicate with your team and establish sensible conclusions with the information and data present. These are the types of educational knowledge and interpersonal skills that will guarantee success.

It's no big secret that professions in areas such as accounting; finance; economics; computer and information sciences; and electrical, mechanical, and computer engineering are the highest demand. These positions will be in high demand because they are in growing industries; they will offer job security and good pay. Those two things make up a good job.

Unfortunately, few American students pursue expertise in STEM fields. Additionally, we have an inadequate pipeline of teachers skilled in those subjects. That's why the US Department of Education has set a priority of increasing the number of students and teachers who are proficient in these vital fields. We need to learn from our past to prepare for the future and avoid setting up the next generation to fail.

America used to be the global educational leaders of the world, but we can no longer claim this title. This is further illustrated in the economics and employment sectors, which spell out that we are in a competitive brain game with the entire world. Younger generations of American students aren't just in competition against one another but also against the students and workers across the globe.

We have been led to believe that America is amongst the leaders in the world in education, but we are *not*! According to the Organization for Economic Cooperation and Development (OECD), the US didn't crack the top ten ranking for science, reading, and math. In reading and science, the US is hovering barely above the OECD average, and in math, we are actually several spots below average.[46] The US has a lot of room to make up, and one place to start is by expanding our efforts in STEM field education.

Help Wanted

61

Majors in the STEM Field

Science

Biology/ Microbiology	Biologist, zoologist, marine biologist, veterinarian, bacteriologist, lawyer, physician, health care professional
Physics	Astrophysicist, statisticians, health physicist, computer programmer, nuclear medical technician
Neuroscience	Anatomist, biomedical engineer, neurologist, neuroscientist, surgeon
Chemistry/ Biochemistry	Pharmacist, physician, research scientist, technical writer, laboratory technician.
Atmospheric Science	Environmentalist, climate researcher, wind power developer, meteorologist, power manager

Technology

Computer Science	Corporate IT specialist, financial analyst, lawyer, network administrator, hardware engineer
Computer Programming	Web designer, computer graphics artist, computer systems engineer, computer programmer
Information Sciences	Software engineer, database administrator, IT manager
Management Information Systems	Operation analyst, quality control manager, director of materials and inventory
Software Engineering	Software creator, software developer, software developer, systems analyst

Engineering

Electrical Engineering	Aerospace engineer, electrical engineer, management consultant, power company manager, production engineer,
Civil Engineering	Civil engineer, materials engineer, waterworks engineer, structural engineer, systems engineer
Computer Engineering	Product developer, robotics, computer network architects, computer systems admin, computer hardware engineer
Mechanical Engineering	Automotive engineer, design engineer, reliability engineer, mechanical engineer
Bioengineering	Bioengineer, biomedical engineer, physician, physiologist, medical consultant
Engineering Technology	Automobile industry, design engineer, digital systems, power generator, systems engineer
Environmental Engineering	Ecologist, environmental lawyer, environmental engineer, pollution control engineer, pollution officer
Nuclear Engineer	Plant designer, plant engineer, radioactive waste manager, nuclear reactor operator, nuclear physicist

Mathematics

Applied Mathematics	Mathematician, research analyst, actuaries, information scientist, postsecondary teacher
Accounting	Accountant, internal auditor, account manager, accounts payable/receivable clerk, budget analyst
Statistics	Statistician, mudlogger, quantitative analyst, researcher, data scientist, optimization analyst
Economics	Economist, financial advisor, investment research analyst, management consultant, market research analyst,
Finance	Corporate banking, investment banking, financial planner, portfolio manager, trader, entrepreneur

Help Wanted

Experts all seem to agree that the job market is changing at an accelerating pace due to the technological, demographic, and socio-economic disruption. The evolving skills that employers desire are shortening the shelf life of employees' existing skills. So, if you think that after graduating with a college degree you will be through with education, think again. Even if you are done with formal education, there is always more to learn to prepare yourself for the next phase of your work life. Constant retraining is something that all companies will be required to accommodate. Disruptive changes to business models will have a profound impact in a rapidly-evolving employment landscape. The ability to anticipate and prepare for future skills requirements is vital to fully seize the opportunities presented by technical trends and hopefully eliminate undesirable outcomes.

I intend to provide you with information that will assist you and hopefully help you understand where you think your future might head, and possibly even develop a game plan as to how to get there. Your world is a lot harder and considerably more complicated than the one previous generations have lived through. The reaction speed to everything is compounded, and the decisions you make now will affect you today, tomorrow, and forever. No need to exert any pressure here, because you have enough pressure already.

My advice to you is to work hard and establish yourself in today's rat race because nothing will be handed to you. Until proven otherwise, my motto will be "fear is my friend." Fear is the uncertainty that is created by the unknown, and it forces us out of our comfort zones, which is essential for personal and professional growth. The solution is to attempt to identify and conquer the unknown. To a large degree, your career choice will determine not only your financial well-being but also your happiness.

When we discuss fields of study, jobs, careers, occupations, and professions, we're not just talking about work, income, status, responsibility, respect, satisfaction, and qualifications. We're talking about where you will spend a vast majority of your time. I hope you realize the importance of this chapter.

Outside of love, the qualities that we strive to achieve including a sense of accomplishment, self-satisfaction, prestige, money, and position will provide you with the essential ingredients for happiness. The categories outlined over the next few pages will help you identify jobs that are becoming more popular due to the growing industries in technology that we have already discussed. I want to recommend to you to review the majors, industries, careers, professions, and occupations carefully, in addition to doing your own research. This only provides you with a menu of options, but if something seems intriguing to you, seek out additional information through your research and by seeking out advice from friends, family, or mentors. Don't be afraid to ask for help. You will be amazed, how many are willing to help.

The accumulated information of employment sectors presented here can be daunting. If I were younger and facing major "what do I want to do" decisions, the professions listed in the STEM fields above would scare me to death. The picture that is sometimes painted is that you need to have a Master's Degree, or a Doctoral Degree or be a physician, a scientist, an engineer, a lawyer or a computer nerd. While it makes life easier, we need to keep in mind that it is not necessarily the degree, but the knowledge and that "success is driven not only by *what* you know but by what *do* with what you know." In Chapter 11, (Me, Myself, and I) it is projected that 40% of the future jobs will be provided by entrepreneurs companies of one that have the knowledge and operate in the back of their garage.

When you find something that you are interested in, be proactive. Take the time to learn more and find ways to gain some experience through an internship or by shadowing someone at work. This will help you determine if you like it before you completely commit to pursuing it.

There's this story I heard about little Johnny. One day his teacher asked him, "Johnny, what do you want to do when you grow up?" Johnny thought about it and answered, "I want to be happy!" I believe this is the perfect answer and the exact advice I give to you! To achieve happiness, it is imperative that you enjoy what you do.

I have attached *the Bureau of Labor Statistics*[47] hyperlink that has outlined 1000's potential careers and areas of study with ten-year projections in mind. This links is the most comprehensive index of career opportunities from A-Z, educational requirements, job descriptions, salary ranges, work environment, experience required, available anywhere. The data found on this website will provide you with excellent information a number of careers that will go a long way in helping you choose a direction that makes you happy.

Please do yourself a favor and if you are reading this in a digital format, click on the *Bureau of Labor Statistics*[47] and it will enlighten you as to your employment options. The occupations are highlighted below and if you are reading this in a paper format, please paste it in your browser and view on your computer as you will not be disappointed.

Occupational Outlook, Highest paying & Fastest Growing Careers

- Architecture and Engineering
- Arts and Design
- Building and Grounds Cleaning
- Business and Financial
- Community and Social Service
- Computer and Information Technology
- Construction and Extraction
- Education, Training, and Library
- Entertainment and Sports
- Farming, Fishing, and Forestry
- Food Preparation and Serving
- Healthcare
- Installation, Maintenance, and Repair
- Legal
- Life, Physical, and Social Science
- Management
- Math
- Media and Communication
- Military
- Office and Administrative Support
- Personal Care and Service
- Production
- Protective Service
- Sales
- Production
- Protective Service
- Sales
- Transportation and Material Moving

While we may not fully understand or have the exact information on the individual jobs that will be available 20 years into the future, this is an educated guess by some of the most brilliant people in the world, that have extensively researched the available options. And even if they are wrong….you will win.

People, Politics, and Problems

C hange occurs at a much slower pace in our politics, society, business, economics, and law than it does in technology. So, while artificial intelligence is rapidly evolving, the world around us is struggling to keep pace.

This wave of automation is reshaping our world and with it drastically altering all political rules and stability. The advancements and changes in computers, medical technology, robotics, cloud storage and the new cryptocurrency effect how we do business in our new economic world. Machines are taking the place of humans in the workplace because of their production capabilities and cost efficiency. Legislation has yet to make the necessary adjustments for an emerging workplace. This is leaving many without jobs and if this trend continues technology has the potential to destroy our economy.

This presents a problem with social, business, and political changes unable to keep up with the acceleration of technological advances. Changes in technology, social environments, business models, and politics are all intertwined, and this tends to compound the problems we face as a world and society. Our lives and how we communicate have and will continue to change with technology. The advancements in computers, medical technology, robotics, cloud storage, and payment systems, all stemming from the development of technology, dramatically affect how we do business which will have a significant impact on our economic world. With growth and change in artificial intelligence and their ability to perform jobs historically provided by humans, the rising unemployment rates will need to be addressed and solved, along with other political issues sure to follow. Unfortunately, the speed at which technology is evolving is putting extra urgency on these issues, and it compounds our need for comprehensive and careful political and economic solutions at every turn.

"Politics is the art of looking for trouble, finding it everywhere, diagnosing it incorrectly, and applying the wrong remedies."

— Groucho Marx

<u>Gerlind Wisskirchen</u>, International Bar Association Global Employment Institute Vice Chair for Multinationals, stated:

> Certainly, technological revolution is not new, but in the past it has been more gradual. What is new about the present revolution is the alacrity with which change is occurring, and the broadness of impact being brought about by AI robotics. Jobs at all levels in society presently undertaken by humans are at risk of being reassigned to robots or AI, and the legislation once in place to protect the rights of human workers may be no longer fit the purpose in some cases.

A new poverty trap is highly likely as unemployment rates climb in a technology-inspired economic system intended to help keep them from earning enough to escape poverty. This dire economic issue will need to be addressed by our political leaders, and it is one of the most severe political problems that will face in this generation. Wisskirchen later stated, "New labor and employment legislation is urgently needed to keep pace with increased automation."[48]

I believe the problem is not so much that there will be no jobs, as we've already discussed some of the growing fields and positions that will become available because of innovation and technological

Morgan

❧

70

growth, but rather an entire generation of people will be unprepared, unable, and unqualified to take over those jobs. The new employment opportunities will be of no value to those being displaced by the machines in the first place because they will not be able to fill those open positions.

According to an Oxford University study, 47 percent of US jobs are threatened by the current "AI Armageddon" of robotics. Large proportions of those put out of work will be in their forties and fifties, still years away from retirement and now being forced to change careers. This is a difficult thing to ask of people in the middle stages of their lives. They most likely aren't looking to redefine their careers, and that is exactly what they are being forced to do. Solutions must be put in place to avoid utter disaster because it will trickle down to other areas of our world.

Politics, public opinion, social change, and business model hierarchies will all be under extreme pressure to change, a commodity that our political world may face challenges with as it adapts.

Again, please understand I am just the messenger here, but this innovative disruption will force the economy to enter into a new era with possibly significant changes. It is possible that the economy will arrive at a point of generating enough profits, in principle, for everyone. Currently, one of the struggles our economy faces is not the overall profit we can generate, but the profit discrepancy. In other words, we often see the rich become richer, and the poor become poorer. So, in this new period, it is not so much about maximizing the income production, but rather about the distribution of wealth and how people get a share of what is produced. It is being projected that everything from trade policies to government projects and commercial regulations will be evaluated in the future by this financial distribution.

One governmental basic program concept that has floated around for years is called Universal Basic Income (UBI). It suggests providing everyone a sufficient income to cover basic living needs regardless of whether or not they are employed.[49] This type of program would take a current salary and give it significantly more impact and value because of the reduced costs of daily living needs. So, while technology is forcing us to reconsider our policies to protect workers better, it also makes these new opportunities possible.

People, Politics, and Problems

71

For example, the innovative disruption we are facing should cause the cost of goods to decrease based on the production efficiency of our robotic manufacturing. In turn, this helps economic welfare programs such as UBI become possible.

However, the UBI program would need to be implemented on a global scale once technological advances spread throughout countries across the world, impacting each's economic system in a trickle effect. However, unanswered questions remain: "What does it cost?" and "Who is going to pay for it?"

To pass an international bill of this magnitude is nearly unimaginable, and I would consider it highly unlikely, seeing the extended, futile, and stalemated political battles in existence with comparatively simple programs. One possible solution could be imposing a tax or fee on robots to help implement this worldwide UBI program. A modern-day example of this is the Hawaii tourist tax, which is distributed to full-time residents of the state.

State programs such as this give hope that innovation is possible in our government. Positive change can be made if we can find the patience, understanding, and compassion to work together and jointly solve our anticipated social, political, and economic problems. Now, this international UBI concept may seem far-fetched, but regardless of how we find the solution, a climbing unemployment rate will need to be addressed.

We are still at the start of this shift, but clearly, politics will change, along with free-market beliefs and social structures. The truth is, we are not sure how things will take shape, but the political climate is light-years behind our technological advancements, and it has some catching up to do. There will be policy changes in the future, but your guess is as good as mine as to what those policies will demand.

As I briefly mentioned in the chapter "Technology Explosion," city's populations are rapidly growing, and part of this is due to technology and the rise of the opportunity it presents in large cities. When we attempt to paint a political picture of what our world might look like twenty to thirty years from now, we need to realize rural life will be almost nonexistent. Cities are where the money is. They control politics, decide the outcomes of political elections, offer job opportunities, control the flow of capital, and create innovation. The largest educational institutions, restaurants, sports facilities, libraries, medical facilities, and entertainment venues are all located in cities.

The dark side of the growing face of worldwide megacities is the almost inevitable development of slums filled with a poverty-stricken population. A slums—aside from the crime and drugs—is defined by Un-Habitat as "a settlement with inadequate access to safe water, sanitation, and other critical infrastructure, as well as poor housing, high population density, and the absence of legal tenure in housing." As of 2016, roughly a billion people across the globe live in what can be defined as a slum, and over the next couple of decades, this number is predicted to grow dramatically for three reasons: a surplus of rural populations looking for work; structural damage from environmental disasters caused by climate change; and future conflicts in the Middle East and Asia over access to natural resources.

In an article from *Quantumrun* titled "Our Future is Urban: Future of Cities P1", David Tal stated:

> Left unchecked, the poor conditions of growing slums can spread outwards, causing a variety of political, economic, and security threats to nations at large. For example, these slums are a perfect breeding ground for organized criminal activity (as seen in the favelas of Rio De Janeiro, Brazil) and terrorist recruitment (as seen in the refugee camps in Iraq and Syria), whose participants can cause havoc in the cities they neighbor. Likewise, the poor public health conditions of these slums are a perfect breeding ground for a range of infectious pathogens to spread outward rapidly. In all, tomorrow's national security threats may originate from those future mega-slums where there's a vacuum of governance and infrastructure.

As our cities continue to grow, our government and legislation must do their best to limit the growth of slum population. Not only is it devastating to those stuck in a bad situation they can't escape but it also could cripple our overall growth as a society, nation, and world.

If people control politics, and cities are where these people live and work, then it follows that the population of the city will explode. The world's population growth in urban areas as is projected by the United Nations that over four hundred cities will be home to over a million people. Urban areas drive the economy, as cities generally have significant influence in local politics, offer a flux of

People, Politics, and Problems

jobs to people of all qualifications, and increasingly encourage the flow of capital between several businesses. The largest educational institutions, restaurants, sports facilities, library, medical facilities and entertainment venues are all located in major cities around the world.

Based on data from the United Nations population study, we have shifted in our living preferences toward density, which is depicted by the below projections:

- Every year, 70 million people join the world's urban population.
- Combined with projected world population growth, 2.5 billion people are expected to settle in urban environments by 2050—with 90 per cent of that growth stemming from Africa and Asia.
- India, China, and Nigeria are expected to make up at least 37 percent of this projected growth, with India adding 404 million urban dwellers, China 292 million, and Nigeria 212 million.
- Thus far, the world's urban population has exploded from just 746 million in 1950 to 3.9 billion by 2014. The global urban population is set to pass 6 billion by 2045.[50]

The more significant factor powering urbanization is the ease and access to everything. Keep in mind that it's not just rural people moving into cities, it's also urbanites moving into ever bigger or better-designed cities. People with specific dreams or employment skill sets are attracted to cities or regions where there are greater opportunities and concentration on their passions—the higher the density of like-minded people, the more opportunities to network and self-actualize professional and personal goals at a faster rate.

For example, a technology or science innovator in the US, regardless of the city they may currently live in, will feel a pull toward tech-friendly cities and regions, such as San Francisco and the Silicon Valley area. Likewise, artists may eventually gravitate toward culturally influential cities, such as New York or Los Angeles. Access and the ability to connect professionally, financially, culturally and socially are fueling the world's booming future of megacities.

Technology has played a significant role in the diversification of the cities which has become a melting pot for cultural diversity, human intelligence, as well as artificial intelligence shaping our world. This cultural revolution has dimmed the distinction between people from all different ethnic backgrounds and formed an integrated network of large cities around the world.

Later in the same article from *QuantumRun*, Tal discusses China's initiative to urbanize their nation. In March 2014, China established a national initiative with the goal to "migrate 60 percent of China's population into cities by 2020. With about 700 million already living in cities, this would involve moving an additional 100 million out of their rural communities into newly built urban developments in less than a decade."

Cities drive the economy at national levels, and local and federal governments alike have sought out to invest in these urban economies' share of tax revenue. Tal goes on in the article to mention the observation of economist Edward Glaeser, "Per-capita incomes in the world's majority-urban societies are four times those of majority-rural societies. And a report by McKinsey and Company stated that growing cities could generate $30 trillion a year into the world economy by 2025." Various studies supporting this trend have shown that doubling a city's population density increases its productivity rate from anywhere between 6 and 28 percent.[51]

While we can debate the difference in the quality of life and happiness in urban settings, there are a great number of people that prefer a quieter, more rural lifestyle over a busy urban jungle. And with transportation technology such as high-speed trains, flying cars and autonomous vehicles, commutes from rural to urban areas are increasingly accessible. However, when comparing the two in terms of access to resources and services, such as access to higher quality schools, hospitals, transportation infrastructure, wealth and diversity of job opportunities, rural areas are perceived to be at a considerable disadvantage.

I personally have experienced the political and social landscape of the big city (Chicago) as well as the rural beauty of the mountains of Utah and the lakes of Michigan. The pulse of our political and financial worlds are controlled by our state and federal governments, which are located in cities. Our cities provide

People, Politics, and Problems

everything from entertainment, restaurants, sports teams, education, job opportunities, family, friends, parties, and fun. I suppose that, in order to be fair, I must also mention traffic, corruption, slums, and crime. The excitement of the city is, and always will be, the center of the world. This is why I love cities and why I hate cities. If the cities are the pulse of our existence, then our getaways are the heart.

The lack of ability our political world has to adapt to rapid changes is extremely concerning. Parties on either side of the aisle are generally controlled by political leaders and individuals who attempt to regulate the status quo while maintaining the existing political hierarchy. We need to balance the sides with a debate that celebrates the virtues of rapid change, agility, and entrepreneurship in consideration of how societies and their citizens cope with and benefit from the considerable turbulence generated by technological change. Globalized productivity and innovation may be beneficial to society, but it could also mean uncertainty in the workforce and financial hardship for many individuals.

It is my prediction that political forces will attempt to control the effects of our technology, and in some cases maybe it should, as controls will undoubtedly be required for the betterment of economies.

This truly is a double-edged sword with controls and restrictions in addition to impediments to progress. Economic issues transcend across political boundaries, and sometimes decisions that protect the workforces can actually destroy it. For example, if it is more profitable to manufacture a product in countries such as India or China rather than in America, then this option must be considered from a business standpoint. Like it or not, we are part of the world's global economy, and we can no longer think only nationally, but instead incorporate economies and workforces throughout the world.

Technologies reach percolates into our business world in many ways, and it will have a significant impact on our economy and the job market. As I've examined in this book, technology can create more jobs than it destroys. What we are unsure about is if the innovation of technology will disrupt jobs only for a short while or if we may be dealing with a long-term problem. We don't know for sure how we will respond to this massive change and if we are unable to adapt, we will be in serious trouble.

Morgan

76

Technological advancements are like a runaway train that cannot and will not stop. It does not make any difference how the government might attempt to handle impediments to political progress in the face of technological changes. Technology is intended to create opportunities, solve issues, reduce the margin of error, increase efficiency, cut costs, reduce waste and increase profits. However, the question of how technological advancements affect the political system's process remains debatable. Fortunately for you, you are being told now to prepare for the future that is rapidly approaching and even already here in many ways.

People, Politics, and Problems

Me, Myself, and I

> ◤
>
> *"People who are crazy enough to think they can change the world are the ones that do."*
>
> —Steve Jobs

Technology opens the door to Entrepreneurial Opportunities. The explosions within the technology section are rapidly creating economic disruptions throughout our world that can devastate our economy. Fortunately, these same disruptions require innovative solutions that can create incredible opportunities. So, many of these problems are being solved by a startup company of one. "Me Myself & I" describes the entrepreneurial world that will make up the majority of our workforce in the years to come. One thing never changes—solve the problem, and you can make a fortune.

The story of Zhang Xin is an inspiration to anyone with the mind of any entrepreneur. Xin grew up poor in China and worked as a factory worker for years until saving enough money to leave her homeland and attend college. After graduating from college, her fortunes changed as she went to work for the investment firm Goldman Sachs. She eventually branched out and started her own property development company known as SOHO, which became wildly successful earning a net worth of roughly $2 billion. Not bad at all!

Or how about the story of Robert Herjavec, a Croatian Canadian businessman and investor who you may know from the television show *Shark Tank*. Herjavec moved to Halifax, Canada, after living and working on a farm with his family in Croatia. After spending his youth in the middle class, he founded his first company in 1990 from the basement of his own home. BRAK Systems, a Canadian integrator of internet security software that he later sold to AT&T Canada in 2000 for $30.2 million.

Have you ever wondered why industry giants so often swallow the minor players? John Warrillow offers up some explanations in his 2010 article "Four Reasons Big Companies Buy Little Ones," featured in *Inc.*:

> Over the past year, Google has bought a company every two weeks, doubling its stated goal of 12 acquisitions a year and tripling its deal flow over that of the previous 12 months. In each case, these acquisitions have been 'strategic' rather than 'financial.' Many large companies are looking to acquisitions as a means of supplementing their growth.
>
> As a business owner, arguably your most attractive exit option is a strategic sale of your business to a larger company. Typically, strategic buyers are willing to pay more for your business than financial buyers (e.g., private equity firms) because they have strategic assets that can increase the value of both your company and theirs. Plus, strategic buyers have deeper pockets than your management team or next of kin, which make them more generous acquirers than your managers or kids.[52]

An example of a massive company buyout is Samsung's acquisition of Viv Labs' Bixby, an AI assistant worth millions in an effort to build up their expertise and credibility in the tech market. And this is just some of the benefits outside of increased profits.

Morgan

Another scenario of success from a startup is the rise and development of Uber, the massive ride-sharing transportation system. It was created and developed by a UCLA dropout and now has become a standard mode of fast and affordable transportation for users of all walks of life.

An entrepreneur looks for problems and then finds a way to deliver valuable solutions. A problem on its own is just a problem. A problem with a solution is an opportunity. To be a successful entrepreneur, you must be able to identify the problems worth investing in. The ones that can return a significant profit.

So, what can make this so challenging? Well, the market doesn't care about an entrepreneur's motives. It doesn't give a hoot about your passions, your loves, or your desires to drive a Ferrari or save the world. If you want to succeed as an entrepreneur, please remember that the only thing the market wants to know is this: What can you do for me?

Fastlane entrepreneurs are committed to providing value, fulfilling needs, and satisfying wants because this is the formula for success. Fortunes are made by solving problems and delivering valuable solutions.

Opportunity to innovatively solve a problem the world faces is out there. If you ever feel alone on your path or been told you'd be crazy to leave the comfort of the corporate world, please realize you could well be on your way to greatness. Almost all the great people in history chose to break the mold and walk their own path. Starting right now, I challenge you to choose your own path and not compromise your beliefs for anyone. Take the first step and never turn back.

The entrepreneur within you has a lot to offer the future world, as startup organizations are the fastest-growing category in the business sector. Increasingly more workers will start and stay in their careers as entrepreneurs. Many of today's entrepreneurs develop their dreams into viable entities with exit strategies that can be converted into incredible wealth through profits or even selling out to larger companies.

Me, Myself, and I

81

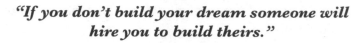

"If you don't build your dream someone will hire you to build theirs."

—Tony Gaskins

Entrepreneurship Opportunity

Technology presents many opportunities for those willing to take risks. Having immediate access to information and research, fast-moving electronic capital, digital data, cloud storage, and quantum computing enables entrepreneurs to compete with big businesses. An entrepreneur's talent and new ideas eliminate the challenge of raising capital. Individuals with talent, ideas, and dreams no longer have an excuse.

An entrepreneur can utilize countless solutions with the help of others just fingertips away from numerous online crowdsourcing resources. Crowdsourcing is an online avenue for seeking and enlisting the help of others on a project or task, with the ability to bring together teams of entrepreneurs. For example, a company called InnoCentive pioneers crowdsourced innovation with an unrivaled global network headquartered in the United States and the United Kingdom. InnoCentive harnesses some 380,000 independent associates, or problem solvers, with PhD-level mind power from around the world who are continually challenged to find solutions for complex problems presented by its members with millions of dollars in rewards available for distribution. This crowdsourcing organization's proven, cost-effective framework for innovation results in problems solved faster than ever before in an entrepreneurial environment with less risk and at a lower cost. With entrepreneur-encouraging platforms, like InnoCentive, any organization, corporation, government, or nonprofit can take advantage of flexible programs geared toward solving complex issues and providing solutions and fresh ideas.

Think of the possibilities. What if, as an entrepreneur, your toughest problem could be solved in thirty to ninety days by tapping into the some of the great minds from around the world? What if it were easier than you ever imagined possible? With an 80 percent success rate, platforms like InnoCentive can present you with the knowledge and solutions you need to bring your new product to market. They have developed an incentivized process for you to get a diverse range of ideas and solutions to help you tackle the toughest problems and develop your products and services. The beauty is that you can play both sides of this equation as either the entrepreneur looking for solutions or one of the individuals providing the solutions.

Charles W. Leadbeater, social entrepreneur and author of The Astral Plane *and social entrepreneur,* stated "Many of the big changes of the next 25 years will come from unknowns working in their bedrooms and garages. And by 2035 we will be talking about the coming of quantum computing, which will take us beyond the world of binary and digital computing."[53] As Leadbeater illustrates, demand is exploding and playing out vividly in today's startup world.

"Optimism is a strategy for making a better future. Because unless you believe that the future can be better, you are unlikely to step up and take responsibility for making it so."

—Noam Chomsky

Another avenue for entrepreneurs to consider is independent employment with companies exploring new technologies. Facebook and Google's development of technologies to place balloons and permanent solar drones at sixty-five thousand feet to blanket the globe with Wi-Fi robots and artificial intelligence that will allow access to "hundreds of expert systems literally waiting in the cloud with answers on any topic, so that the solutions to the problems of improving our personal lives and our businesses will be limited only by our imagination in asking the questions. And we'll be able to

Me, Myself, and I

direct those AI experts to work together to come up with powerful, novel solutions. The cross-fertilization of technologies will soar!" Uber, Amazon, eBay, Airbnb, Google, and Facebook are just a few organizations utilizing robotic and AI technology, but there are thousands of relatively unknown smaller start-ups that employ hundreds of thousands of workers and generate tremendous benefits and income for their independently employed workers and entrepreneurs.

> *"Twenty years from now you will be more disappointed by the things you didn't do than by the ones you did."*
>
> —Mark Twain—

To a large extent, we can accomplish entrepreneur success because we no longer have to raise vast amounts of capital to acquire the IT infrastructure necessary to run a business or test out a new business model. *The Economist* magazine puts it in a special report, "Digital startups are bubbling up in an astonishing variety of services and products, penetrating every nook and cranny of the economy. They are reshaping entire industries ..."[54] Technologies such as online data clouds are minimizing storage and access barriers and unleashing entrepreneurial energies in the process. Cloud models are becoming a large piece of the big, big, big picture in an increasingly powerful force of new technologies in the entrepreneur world.

MIT Sloan School of Management professor Thomas Malone stated in his book, *The Future of Work* (pg. 4), that new technologies are changing the entrepreneur world. "Dispersed physically but connected by technology, workers are now able, on a scale never before even imaginable, to make their own decisions using information gathered from many other people and places ... For the first time in history, technologies allow us to gain the economic benefits of

Morgan

84

large organizations, like economies of scale and knowledge, without giving up the human benefits of small ones, like freedom, creativity, motivation, and flexibility."[55] Talk about leveling the playing field for business ventures in all areas. This is it for entrepreneurs!

Along the same lines, Christie Lindor, a management consultant author of *The MECE Muse* (Mutually Exclusive, Collectively Exhaustive), hosts an organization of independent consultants who work alongside a growing number of independent contractors to help solve complex business problems. This process is considered a "gig economy" and was created specifically for undergraduate or graduate students interested in a consulting career. Both new and experienced professionals can seek independent consultant work through these types of organizations. In a *TIME* magazine article, Kristen Bahler stated that the individuals "act like talent agents, tasked with helping freelancers find and market their projects." In the article, Bahler quotes Lindor saying these individuals will act as entrepreneurs with "contractual 'micro' projects of varying lengths of time instead of the full time, permanent jobs of today."[56]

Nothing is untouchable, and nothing is outside your realm of possibilities. It used to take a great deal of capital to launch a new start-up, but today you can start up a business right in your living room.

Here's another big asset for those entrepreneurs: start-up incubator organizations. For example, Y Combinator is one of the world's most powerful start-up incubator companies that has helped spawn more than a thousand companies by funding capital support or seed money. Aspiring entrepreneurs can find financial support from companies like Y Combinator. The majority of entrepreneur visionaries like Tesla Motors, Uber, Airbus, Dropbox, Intel, and Cisco were brought together by the brightest minds of entrepreneurial zeal, offers inspirational through their success for future entrepreneurs. The United States leads the world in innovation across a range of industries partly due to the infrastructure and financial support from companies like Y Combinator. This levels the playing field for all entrepreneurs looking to stand out from the crowd and change the world. Technology is continuing to make it easier than ever to become an entrepreneur and boost growth to create healthy micro-economies.

Me, Myself, and I

85

> *"Don't be afraid to assert yourself, have confidence in your abilities and don't let the bastards get you down."*
>
> — Michael Bloomberg, Founder Bloomberg LP

AI advancements are driving improvements across nearly every marketplace sector. Technology is embedded in entire business models and distribution networks, improving search engine functionality, shipping and delivery predictions, fraud detection, and risk management. Artificial intelligence is used to examine and determine which sellers are most trustworthy and how to best promote businesses to provide better customer experiences. Additionally, AI is embedded in our work on pricing and insights for our inventory. With AI assistance, entrepreneurs can operate, compete, and succeed in the business world, even when starting on a small platform.

Take Tanya Crew, for example. Formerly a struggling single mother trying to finish college, Crew first started selling motorcycle accessories on eBay to make extra money. She went on to build a successful online business and was able to employ two other entrepreneurs. AI-driven technology will help small, independent businesses like these to optimize item pricing, predict shifts in consumer behavior, and much more.

Another great example is Mohammed Taushif Ansari, who moved to Mumbai with a dream of starting a business that created and exported leather garments. With just a sewing machine and a laptop, he began selling his products worldwide on eBay's platform. He later developed his dream into an online retail business that exports to thirty countries and employs ten people. His products are also now shown to customers on social platforms via eBay's AI-powered ShopBot. Online platforms such as eBay have directly helped businesses like Ansari's optimize their product listings and images to attract varying types of consumers.

Want to develop a talent that could make you a lot of money? You might think this is impossible, but there are countless entrepreneur opportunities right at your fingertips. It's predicted that by 2040 over 40 percent of the workforce will be entrepreneurs. Therefore, there is a 40 percent probability that entrepreneurship will be in your future. So open yourself up to the possibilities and prepare yourself to achieve the impossible!

Chapter

Love Really Does Makes the World Go 'Round

"It's impossible," said pride. "It's risky," said experience. "It's pointless," said reason. "It's the wrong time," said logic. "It's not good," said dignity. "Give it a try," whispered the heart."

—Ja Nasia Richardson

Education can bring us intelligence. Technology can increase our efficiency. Knowledge can provide us with jobs. Money can buy us things. Exercise can make us strong. Medicine can give us good health and a long life. But love is the only thing that can satisfy the heart, and that makes us truly happy. Love leaves us wanting more and running in circles to get it.

You might be thinking, "What does my love life have to do with technology?" But please keep in mind, we can't discuss your future without recognizing how technology will affect how we live and love.

Life without love would be like the computer without the software. The computer with its motherboard with all its circuit, processors, monitors and hard drive equipment would be useless without the software. Technology is providing great opportunities, but love gives our lives meaning, and I would hate for you to be incredibly successful but unhappy.

You may think you have all the answers and your life planned out perfectly. You may even believe you are sufficiently prepared for everything the world will throw at you. However, without love, you may always be searching for more. A life without love is a life without meaning.

Relationships and Technology

One of the wonderful advantages of living in our present world is that technology makes it so easy to communicate with anyone at any time. This provides the opportunity for us to build relationships with friends all around the world. Avenues of communication have opened up opportunities previously unimaginable.

Technology can also affect the way we view our relationships. In the article "Can Love Survive in the Age of Technology?," Randi Gunther, PhD and relationship therapist, states:

> I am both fascinated and concerned about technology's potential to outpace the success of intimate relationships. If we are constantly seduced into procuring the latest innovations in ever-more-amazing technological gadgetry, how can we not want the same continuous novelty in our personal relationships? And, if so, how do we even consider living in a long term relationship where innovative discovery naturally diminishes over time? It would seem that sequential, revolving-door relationships should serve the purpose of ever-new experiences that hold our interest.[58]

Loving People

> *"Love is not finding someone to live with.*
> *It's finding someone you can't live without."*
>
> —Rafael Ortiz

When we think about love, we typically associate that with finding a life partner. The love between two people in marriage, committed to each other in a special bond, is like nothing else on earth. I've been married to my college sweetheart for over fifty years, and while it hasn't always been easy, it has been an incredible journey that I could not imagine my world without her.

And while marriage is arguably the greatest form of love there is, love can be found most anywhere. Our connection with others is what makes this life so special. Whether that's your spouse, your siblings, your friends, your parents, your children or whoever else in the world you have a great love for, even your dog. There is nothing greater than experiencing love.

Listen to the words of Anaïs Nin, a pre-World War II romantic author who seventy-five years ago realized the importance of being connected with people and technology's threat against the concept of love. "This is the illusion which might cheat us of being in touch deeply with the one breathing next to us, the dangerous time when mechanical voices, radios, telephones take the place of human intimacies and the concept of being in touch with millions brings a greater and greater poverty in intimacy and human vision."

We are not meant to go through life alone. When you accomplish something, significant or small, it's better when your loved ones are there to celebrate with you. When you fall again and again and can't seem to get up, your loved ones will be there to pick you up, care for you, and encourage you to keep going. When you have a challenging and life-altering decision, your loved ones are there to help you make the right choices. And the same should be done in reverse. Always be there for those you care for. Whether they need your support, your help, or just your ears to listen.

Love is powerful. Not just the love you have in your own heart but the love someone else has for you and how that can give life. Love gives you the freedom to be yourself, confidence when you have none, and peace in the middle of a storm. As the world transitions to becoming more dependent on technology, I hope you find ways to use technology to enhance your relationships, not destroy them.

Loving Yourself

The world of technology moves fast, and it has caused us to speed up our lives as well. Because of this, we often can miss out on some of the greatest things life has to offer. Take the advice of Ferris Bueller when he says, "Life moves pretty fast. If you don't stop and look around once in a while, you could miss it." So, please, enjoy life's experiences. In the song "Thinking Out Loud" by Ed Sheeran he says, "Kiss me under the light of a thousand stars." I don't think today's, or tomorrow's, technology can compete with that. Try it; I think you'll like it!

The *Washington Post* conducted a social experiment in a Washington, DC, metro station. They hired famous violinist Joshua Bell, disguised him as a homeless man, and had him perform six pieces of Johann Sebastian Bach—some of the most incredible classical music ever written. Thousands of people passed through and heard Bell playing, but only a few briefly stopped to listen, and six people left a small donation. Everyone else was moving too quickly to appreciate the musical masterpiece taking place right in front of them.[59]

Our lives have been excessively compromised when we do not have time to stop and listen to one of the best musicians playing some of the best music ever written. If we can't stop to enjoy a few moments, then how many other things are we missing? Life moves quickly, and we need to learn to stop and smell the roses, appreciate our world, and listen to the music.

Back from the Future

> 💬
>
> *"I skate to where the puck is going to be, not where it's been."*
>
> —Wayne Gretzky

Road Map to Tomorrow examines the scientific advancements currently taking place. More importantly, this book studies, evaluates, and predicts the changing technologies that lie ahead. If "knowledge itself is power," as infamous English professor Sir Francis Bacon pointed out, then the knowledge provided in this book will power the vision for your future.

Envision this book like the movie *Back to The Future*. I'm Marty McFly, and I have just traveled back from the future to assist you in planning and preparing for your future. It's like going into a final exam knowing ahead of time the questions that will be on the test. It's much easier to study when you know *what* to study.

By no means am I attempting to make your decisions for you or tell you what to do regarding the rest of your life, as your future rests in your own hands. In my attempt to provide you with this future road map, we need to ask ourselves this question: What are the best potential options for a successful future? Position yourself in the right place at the right time, with the proper knowledge, and you are setting yourself up for success.

Whether you are just starting your journey or you're a seasoned veteran, getting off on the right foot has many advantages. By studying the disciplines, concepts, and innovations, we have discussed throughout this book. Or as Wayne Gretzky might say, skate to where our world economy, job market, and technology is going to be, not where it has been.

As a true sense of the "back from the future" theme of this chapter, I would like to introduce you to a friend I made from the future, Captain Morgan. Captain Morgan is my robotic assistant. We know robotic assistants like Alexa and Watson, but in the future, these artificial intelligent assistants function like a life-like friend. Via a simple digital chip embedded into our bodies, robotic assistants can evaluate and monitor everything from medical conditions, financial portfolios, social lives, to even schedules.

The reason I want to introduce you to this AI possibility is twofold. First, if Watson, Siri, or Alexa can read and retain 100 percent of the millions of pages written about cancer, or renewable energy, or any subject for that matter, then I no longer need to be the smartest person in the room. All I need is to have a robotic assistant with a chip implanted into my brain that can access Captain Morgan's expertise and poof—I'm brilliant! If we think about where we are heading, it appears reasonable that our future intelligence can be developed through technology and utilized by everyone to develop nearly anything.

Just twenty years ago, if you had a question pop into your head, I wouldn't be able to access the answer without consulting an expert on the subject or going to the library and searching through books to find it myself. Now we pull out our phones and have the answer in seconds. If this type of advancement happened over the past twenty years, imagine the possibilities over the next twenty years, when we have already learned so much more about technology.

It is entirely within reason to expect Captain Morgan to not just merely search the internet and provide information about the news or weather but also help operate a business, make meaningful life decisions, and perform daily physical tasks for us like exploring

Morgan

healthcare alternatives, planning a vacation, and buying clothes, using human-like intelligence.

But what makes this intelligence potentially even more significant than ours is that it also relies on algorithms to access any information or program at any time, becoming an expert in an instant. For example, if you wanted to explore financial investments, Captain Morgan could continually monitor millions of transactions, all financial news, income tax codes, live trading data and then invest your money based on all your personal and pertinent investment data, financial circumstances and attitude toward risk behaviors. Captain Morgan is just one of many examples of how our futures can be helped with AI assistance.

Prepare for Change

Additionally, I've emphasized how the speed and efficiency of technology are increasing. The rapid increase in technology changes and efficiency in areas of production, manufacturing, logistics, sales, marketing, and management are all causes for innovative economic disruption affects your future career prospects, your love life, and even where you wind up living.

Technology cycles have begun to outpace business model cycles that shape our world. We need to learn to manage the innovative disruption, not strive for stability. Disruptions and innovations cause change, and you either change with the times or get left behind. There are no guarantees that today will look like yesterday, or that tomorrow will look like today. Our world is changing rapidly, and old rules no longer apply.

My previous book, *Kernels of Knowledge*, presented the principals of determining where you are, what you want to do, and how to get there. Writing this book led me to think more about the directional decisions you make in your life. Determining your future path is not easy and requires a lot of soul-searching. I hope that this book will help you tackle some of the decisions you face.

Many of the roads to your future aren't built yet, and most of those that have been built are not in a straight line. The directions we take arc very seldom without changes. Most require detours and pit stops along the way. Your educational selections may change, your career choices may change, and the opportunities presented to you throughout life will change. The only constant is *change* itself.

We are entering a time when change is happening at a faster rate than ever before. The only way you will succeed is by developing the ability to adapt and solve the problems that will come your way.

Pursue Your Passions

"There are many things in life that will catch your eye, but only few will catch your heart. Pursue these"

—Michael Nolan, UK High Court judge

Pretend for a second that you are a wealthy king or queen and the world is in your hands. You have no real constraints as to ability, finance, or educational credentials. You've followed the advice presented in this book. Now, where do you envision yourself? What are you doing in our future world? What are your dreams? What are your passions?

We only get one life, and that can either cause you to live cautiously, always playing it safe, or live freely, with nothing to lose. I hope you get to live the latter. Don't let fear stop you. Don't let finances stop you. Don't let the world stop you. If you have a dream, then chase it. Our world is exciting, and it presents an abundance of opportunities that we have never seen before. It's all up to you, as you are entirely in control.

You have specific talents, skills, and interests that make you who you are. You are unique, and you can provide the world something that nobody else can. If you are not sure what your passions are, keep searching, they are there, look harder, and you will find them. Take time every day to do some soul-searching.

Once you find your greatest passions, follow them. You never know where they will lead you.

"Shoot for the moon. Even if you miss you will land among the stars."

—Norman Vincent Peale

The future is now!

Note from the Author

Dear Friends,

The adjustments that Generations X, Y, and Z are facing in their lifetimes are unprecedented and located in unchartered waters. Technological innovations will affect everything, and constant change has and will continue to be the new normal.

In past years, problem solving required mankind to spend hundreds of hours researching in libraries, reading books, magazines, articles, interviewing professionals, and studying volumes of data in encyclopedias Today we simply look inside the cloud or asking personal artificial intelligence assistants such as Alexa, Suri, Cortana, or Watson to provide us with immediate answers to whatever questions we might have.

We are approaching an unstoppable information evolution that is smarter, faster, more fluid, and thanks to the rise of quantum computing, will solve complex problems regarding our environment, aging, disease, poverty, famine, space exploration, and possibly even war.

While theories and predictions are helpful, the scope of challenges upcoming workforce-age generations face is insurmountable. And we have no idea how these generations will handle the most exciting, powerful, and even scary knowledge being discovered. However, I hope that your technological future will continue to improve and protect our world and the people in it.

Good Luck,

John *Morgan* Mullen

Sources

1. "Going Beyond Beliefs." *Nirvana: Absolute Freedom*, by Yogi Kanna, Kamath, 2011, pp. 7.
2. Straw, John, and Michael Baxter. "Prologue." *IDisrupted*, New Generation Publishing, 2014, p. 13.
3. "Human Genome Project." *Wikipedia*, Wikimedia Foundation, 16 July 2018, en.wikipedia.org/wiki/Human_Genome_ Project.
4. Zimmermann, Kim Ann. "History of Computers: A Brief Timeline." *LiveScience*, Purch, 6 Sept. 2017, www.livescience. com/20718-computer-history.html.
5. "The Centre for Computing History." *Centre For Computing History*, www.computinghistory.org.uk/det/1078/Tommy-Flowers/.
6. "Computer." *Wikipedia*, Wikimedia Foundation, 23 July 2018, en.wikipedia.org/wiki/Computer.
7. Lawson, Stephen. "Networks in 2020: More Traffic, Less Energy." *PCWorld*, PCWorld, 13 May 2013, www.pcworld.com/ article/2038602/networks-in-2020-more-traffic-less-energy.html.
8. Gaudin, Sharon. "Intel: Chips in Brains Will Control Computers by 2020." *Computerworld*, Computerworld, 19 Nov. 2009, www. computerworld.com/article/2521888/app-development/ intel--chips-in-brains-will-control-computers-by-2020.html.
9. Nardelli, Michele. "Film Coating Transforms Contact Lenses into Computer Screens." *Phys.org - News and Articles on Science and Technology*, Phys.org, phys.org/news/2016-02-coating-contact-lenses-screens.html.

10. "Robotic Industries Association." *Robotics Online*, www.robotics. org/robotics/industrial-robot-industry-and-all-it-entails.

11. "The First Industrial Robot (1954 – 1961)." *About History of Information.com*, www.historyofinformation.com/expanded. php?id=4071.

12. "IDC Unveils Its Top 10 Predictions for Worldwide Robotics for 2017 and Beyond." *IDC: The Premier Global Market Intelligence Company*, www.idc.com/getdoc. jsp?containerId=prAP42000116.

13. Hanson, Robin. *The Age of Em: Work, Love, and Life When Robots Rule the Earth*. Oxford University Press, 2018.

14. Branco, Jorge. "Robots to Replace Almost Half of Jobs over next 20 Years: Expert." *The Sydney Morning Herald*, The Sydney Morning Herald, 23 Mar. 2015, www.smh.com.au/ technology/robots-to-replace-almost-half-of-jobs-over-next-20-years-expert-20150323-1m5oei.html.

15. Lautman, Mark. *When the Boomers Bail: a Community Economic Survival Guide*. Logan Square Press, 2011.

16. Manyika, James, et al. "Harnessing Automation for a Future That Works." *McKinsey & Company*, Jan. 2017, www.mckinsey. com/featured-insights/digital-disruption/harnessing-automation-for-a-future-that-works.

17. Chui, Michael, et al. "Where Machines Could Replace Humans--and Where They Can't (Yet)." *McKinsey & Company*, July 2016, www.mckinsey.com/business-functions/digital-mckinsey/our-insights/where-machines-could-replace-humans-and-where-they-cant-yet.\

18. Ro, Isaac. "The Cloud Can Help Cure Cancer: Goldman Sachs' Isaac Ro." *YouTube*, Goldman Sachs, 22 Feb. 2016, www. youtube.com/watch?v=KqMQqT_Zwb0.

19. Drucker, Dr. Ronald P. "Stem Cells Discovered to Be The Superheroes of Healing, Which You May Now Utilize!" *Dr Ron Drucker*, 7 Feb. 2018, drrondrucker.com/blog/2017/05/18/ stem-cells-have-emerged-as-the-new-superheroes-of-healing-which-you-may-now-utilize/.

20. Standaert, Michael. "Blood Test for Early Cancer Detection." *MIT Technology Review*, MIT Technology Review, 8 July 2015, www.technologyreview.com/s/534991/liquid-biopsy/.

21. Bertalan, Dr. Meskó. "Nanotechnology in Healthcare: Getting Smaller and Smarter." *The Medical Futurist*, 15 Dec. 2016, medicalfuturist.com/getting-smaller-and-smarter-nanotechnology-in-healthcare/.

22. Osagie, Phil. "Can Future Heart Attacks Be Prevented? Science & Medicine Race the Clock." *Quantumrun*, 23 Apr. 2017, www.quantumrun.com/article/can-future-heart-attacks-be-prevented-science-medicine-race-clock.

23. Peterson, Kyle. "The Gene Editors Are Only Getting Started." *The Wall Street Journal*, Dow Jones & Company, 7 July 2017, www.wsj.com/articles/the-gene-editors-are-only-getting-started-1499461756.

24. Koort, Bob. "What If I Told You..." *Goldman Sachs*, www.goldmansachs.com/our-thinking/pages/what-if-i-told-you-full/?playlist=0.

25. Boroujerdi, Robert D., et al. *What If I Told You...*, Goldman Sachs, 2 Dec. 2015, www.goldmansachs.com/our-thinking/pages/macroeconomic-insights-folder/what-if-i-told-you/report.pdf.

26. Tracy, Sam. "Driverless Cars Will Reshape the Economy, but These Three Hurdles Will Make It a Slow Process." *The Huffington Post*, TheHuffingtonPost.com, 19 June 2016, www.huffingtonpost.com/sam-tracy/driverless-cars-will-resh_b_7625238.html.

27. Kanter, Zack. "How Uber's Autonomous Cars Will Destroy 10 Million Jobs And Reshape The Economy by 2025." *CBS San Francisco*, CBS San Francisco, 27 Jan. 2015, sanfrancisco.cbslocal.com/2015/01/27/how-ubers-autonomous-cars-will-destroy-10-million-jobs-and-reshape-the-economy-by-2025-lyft-google-zack-kanter/.

28. "World Urbanization Prospects - Population Division." *United Nations*, United Nations, esa.un.org/unpd/wup/Download/.

Sources

29. "Space Shuttle Challenger Disaster." *Wikipedia*, Wikimedia Foundation, 31 July 2018, en.wikipedia.org/wiki/Space_Shuttle_Challenger_disaster.

30. "Metals.com Announces World's First Asteroid Mining Metals Fund." *PR Newswire: News Distribution, Targeting and Monitoring*, PRNewswire, www.prnewswire.com/news-releases/metalscom-announces-worlds-first-asteroid-mining-metals-fund-300569855.html.

31. Lin, Jeffrey, and P.W. Singer. "A Look at China's Most Exciting Hypersonic Aerospace Programs." *Popular Science*, Popular Science, 18 Apr. 2017, www.popsci.com/chinas-hypersonic-technology.

32. Fox News. "Five Future Transportation Technologies That Will Actually Happen." *Fox News*, FOX News Network, 27 Nov. 2013, www.foxnews.com/tech/2013/11/27/five-future-transportation-technologies-that-will-actually-happen.html.

33. "Fossil." *Department of Energy*, www.energy.gov/science-innovation/energy-sources/fossil.

34. "What Is Clean Energy?" *What Is Clean Energy?—Future Sparks*, www.futuresparks.org.au/why-we-need-clean-energy/what-is-clean-energy.aspx.

35. "Top 6 Things You Didn't Know About Solar Energy." *Department of Energy*, www.energy.gov/articles/top-6-things-you-didnt-know-about-solar-energy.

36. "Top 10 Things You Didn't Know About Wind Power." *Department of Energy*, www.energy.gov/eere/wind/articles/top-10-things-you-didnt-know-about-wind-power.

37. Desjardins, Jeff. "Infographic: The Alternative Energy Sources of the Future." *Visual Capitalist*, 20 Oct. 2016, www.visualcapitalist.com/alternative-energy-sources-future/.

38. "Top 10 Things You Didn't Know about Hydropower." *Department of Energy*, www.energy.gov/articles/top-10-things-you-didnt-know-about-hydropower.

39. "Marine and Hydrokinetic Energy Research & Development." *Department of Energy*, www.energy.gov/eere/water/marine-and-hydrokinetic-energy-research-development.

40. "5 Fast Facts About Nuclear Energy." *Department of Energy*, www.energy.gov/ne/articles/5-fast-facts-about-nuclear-energy.

41. "Nuclear Reactor." *Wikipedia*, Wikimedia Foundation, 3 Aug. 2018, en.wikipedia.org/wiki/Nuclear_reactor.

42. "Nuclear Reactor Technologies." *Department of Energy*, www.energy.gov/ne/nuclear-reactor-technologies.

43. Bessen, James. *Learning by Doing the Real Connection between Innovation, Wages, and Wealth*. Yale University Press, 2015.

44. Hullinger, Jessica. "This Is The Future Of College." *Fast Company*, Fast Company, 20 May 2015, www.fastcompany.com/3046299/this-is-the-future-of-college.

45. "Future of Colleges & Universities – Futurist Thomas Frey." *Futurist Speaker Thomas Frey*, www.futuristspeaker.com/extended-bio/future-of-colleges-universities-futurist-thomas-frey/.

46. "PISA 2015 Results (Volume I) | READ Online." *OECD ILibrary*, read.oecd-ilibrary.org/education/pisa-2015-results-volume-i_9789264266490-en.

47. "Home : Occupational Outlook Handbook:" *U.S. Bureau of Labor Statistics*, U.S. Bureau of Labor Statistics, 13 Apr. 2018, www.bls.gov/ooh/.

48. Wisskirchen, Gerlind. "Law Requires Reshaping as AI and Robotics Alter Employment, States New IBA Report." *IBA - North Korea: Inquiry Finds Kim Jong-Un Should Be Investigated and Prosecuted for Crimes against Humanity*, IBA, www.ibanet.org/Article/NewDetail.aspx?ArticleUid=012a3473-007f-4519-827c-7da56d7e3509.

49. "Basic Income." *Wikipedia*, Wikimedia Foundation, 5 Aug. 2018, en.wikipedia.org/wiki/Basic_income.

50. "World Urbanization Prospects - Population Division." *United Nations*, United Nations, esa.un.org/unpd/wup/Download/.

51. Tal, David. "Our Future Is Urban: Future of Cities P1." *Quantumrun*, 1 Mar. 2017, www.quantumrun.com/prediction/our-future-urban-future-cities-p1.

52. Warrillow, John. "4 Reasons Big Companies Buy Little Ones." *Inc.com*, Inc., 1 Nov. 2010, www.inc.com/articles/2010/11/why-big-companies-buy-small-ones.html.

53. Leadbeater, C. W. *Astral Plane*. Nabu Press, 2010.

54. "A Cambrian Moment." *The Economist*, The Economist Newspaper, 17 Jan. 2014, www.economist.com/special-report/2014/01/17/a-cambrian-moment.

Sources

55. Malone, Thomas W. *The Future of Work: How the New Order of Business Will Shape Your Organization, Your Management Style, and Your Life*. Harvard Business School Press, 2007.

56. Bahler, Kristen. "These Are the Jobs Everyone Will Compete for In the Future | Money." *Time*, Time, 17 Oct. 2017, time.com/money/4982643/6-future-jobs/.

57. "World Urbanization Prospects - Population Division." *United Nations*, United Nations, esa.un.org/unpd/wup/Download/.

58. Gunther, Randi. "Can Love Survive in the Age of Technology?" *Psychology Today*, Sussex Publishers, www.psychologytoday.com/us/blog/rediscovering-love/201103/can-love-survive-in-the-age-technology.

59. Weingarten, Gene. "Pearls Before Breakfast: Can One of the Nation's Great Musicians Cut through the Fog of a D.C. Rush Hour? Let's Find out." *The Washington Post*, WP Company, 8 Apr. 2007, www.washingtonpost.com/lifestyle/magazine/pearls-before-breakfast-can-one-of-the-nations-great-musicians-cut-through-the-fog-of-a-dc-rush-hour-lets-find-out/2014/09/23/8a6d46da-4331-11e4-b47c-f5889e061e5f_story.html?utm_term=.c6214b522827.

About the Author

John ***Morgan*** Mullen is president of the Morgan Group, Inc., a residential real estate development company. By visiting the Morgan Group's website at www.morgangroupdev.com, you'll gain insight into his professional background and accomplishments, which include more than thirty years of experience in the acquisition, financing, development, and disposition of assets acquired through various companies, partnerships, and joint ventures.

His educational credentials include a bachelor's in communication arts from Michigan State University, where he was a quarterback on the 1965 and 1966 national championship football teams. His athletic accomplishments are equally important in shaping him as his educational credentials. While he certainly is not downplaying the value and benefits received from his formal education, the experience attained through playing sports included leadership, teamwork, developing a game plan, dedication and hard work are the life's lessons he incorporated in his first book, *Kernels of Knowledge*. This powerful book walks you through how to achieve your dreams and is available on Amazon.

Morgan's entrepreneurial life has been filled with adventure, change, and the risk of stepping into the unknown. His second book, *Road Map to Tomorrow,* outlines the technologies and challenges that you will face and how best to utilize expert projections to provide you with a map for your future.

Morgan

Recommended Reading

(Show and Tell)

The entertainment and educational value of this book can be verified throughout the many sources identified, including books, articles, internet sources, and videos. Additionally, the depth of the information far exceeds the ability of any one person. For your convenience, hyperlinks are highlighted throughout this section of the book and indexed in this chapter to provide you with more detailed and in-depth data for your comprehensive review. Please keep in mind that in general, mathematical calculations and proven data, along with projections and studies from existing and ongoing research have been exemplified in this book to arrive at future forecasts and predictions.

Introduction

1. Gen-Z Video series http://www.goldmansachs.comhttps://www.thoughtco.com/what-is-a-quantum-computer-2699359/our-thinking/pages/what-if-i-told-you-full/index.html?videoId=141042
2. *Nirvana : Absolute Freedom,* Yogi Kanna, a spiritual author
3. Education, Immigration and business is borderless https://www.youtube.com/watch?v=Qty1xqvQBrA).

Chapter 1
Technology Explosion

1. <u>iDistruped</u>, *Michael Baxter, author* https://www.amazon.com/ iDisrupted-Michael-Baxter-ebook/dp/B00PFYZORA/ ref=sr_1_1?ie=UTF8&qid=1512487251&sr=8-1&keywords=idisrupted

2. Bit Coins Black Chain and the economy of the future… https:// blockgeeks.com/guides/what-is-blockchain-technology/

3. Technology Driving Innovation video http://www. goldmansachs.com/our-thinking/pages/david-solomon-technology-landscape.html

4. These 12 technologies will drive our economic future https:// www.washingtonpost.com/news/wonk/wp/2013/05/24/ these-12-technologies-will-drive-our-economic-future/?utm_ term=.63e1c199c820

5. Disruptive technologies: Advances that will transform life (https://www.mckinsey.com/business-functions/digital-mckinsey/our-insights/disruptive-technologies)

6. The Fourth Industrial Revolution: what it means, how to respond https://www.weforum.org/agenda/2016/01/ the-fourth-industrial-revolution-what-it-means-and-how-to-respond

7. Amazon Concedes Defeat Retail Stores adapt to on-line sales http://banyanhill.com/amazon-concedes-defeat/

8. Most Bizarre Drones video of 10 Drone uses in existence now https://www.youtube.com/watch?v=qlx_wnfnPYg

9. Blockchain could disrupt everything http://www. goldmansachs.com/our-thinking/pages/what-if-i-told-you-full/index.html?videoId=141040

Recommended Reading

Chapter 2
The Intelligence of Artificial Intelligence

1. Video (4:29) that predict many of the new technologies to be developed between now and 2045 https://youtu.be/H2TFXWapQ6c
2. 7 Amazing technologies we'll see by 2030 http://www.businessinsider.com/technologies-future-2030-world-economic-forum-tech-video-2017-2
3. Jennifer Tejada, CEO, PagerDuty *The Defining Tech Trends of the Next Decade* http://www.goldmansachs.com/our-thinking/pages/picc-2016.html
4. 3-D Printing's Exponential Growth https://banyanhill.com/3-d-printings-exponential-growth/
5. The World's Leading Nations for Innovation and Technology http://www.citylab.com/tech/2011/10/worlds-leading-nations-innovation-and-technology/224/)
6. What Will the Next 20 Years Bring? By Babak Hodjat http://www.huffingtonpost.com/babak-hodjat/artificial-intelligence-w_1_b_8894418.html
7. *The Second Wave of Transformation* by John Mauldin,
8. *Physics of the Future*, written by Michio Kaku
9. *Artificial Intelligence*, Stewart Russell, author
10. *The Singularity is Near* by Ray Kurzweil http://www.singularity.com/aboutthebook.html
11. *The Pace of Technology Adoption is Speeding Up*
12. *The Pace of Technology Adoption is Speeding Up* by Rita Gunther McGrath
13. https://hbr.org/2013/11/the-pace-of-technology-adoption-is-speeding-up
14. Inevitable advancement for just the next few years http://www.businessinsider.com/technologies-future-2030-world-economic-forum-tech-video-2017-2
15. Interesting statistics & GRAPHs regarding population, jobs, age in the future http://www.bbc.com/future/story/20170330-5-numbers-that-will-define-the-next-100-years?ocid=ww.social.link.email

16. What humans will evolve into http://www.quantumrun.com/ podcast/episodes/human-evolution-into-computers-by-2070-s1e1-life-in-2030-podcast/
17. *"The Age of Em"* Robin Hanson, an associate professor of economics at George Mason
18. Your addictive, magical, augmented life; What is Augmented Reality, Anyway? http://www.quantumrun.com/prediction/ your-addictive-magical-augmented-life-future-internet-p6
19. The tidal wave of information: The new media age http:// www.quantumrun.com/article/tidal-wave-information-new-media-age
20. New haptic technology moves away from physical touch controls http://www.quantumrun.com/article/new-haptic-technology-moves-away-physical-touch-controls
21. The potential effects of artificial intelligence http:// www.quantumrun.com/article/potential-effects-artificial-intelligence
22. Future World 2030: Dr Michio Kaku's author of *Physics of the Future* predictions (58 Minute Video). https://www.youtube. com/watch?v=OtW6o9i1yWY
23. Cloud can Cure Cancer http://www.goldmansachs. com/our-thinking/pages/what-if-i-told-you-full/index. html?videoId=141418
24. The Value of digital transformation could be as high as $100 trillion over the next decade http://reports.weforum.org/ digital-transformation/identifying-value-at-stake-for-society-and-industry/
25. Quantumrun is a consulting agency that specializes in long-term strategic forecasting and planning. We help companies see around corners by revealing how today's trends might impact their business tomorrow. http://www.quantumrun. com/ http://www.quantumrun.com/future-timeline

Recommended Reading

111

Chapter 3
Quantum Computing

1. Contact Lens technology https://phys.org/news/2017-04-bio-sensing-contact-lens-blood-glucose.html

2. Contact lens screens https://phys.org/news/2016-02-coating-contact-lenses-screens.html

3. Gestures, holograms, and matrix-style mind uploading: Future of computers P3 http://www.quantumrun.com/prediction/gestures-holograms-and-matrix-style-mind-uploading-future-computers-p3

4. *Quantum Computers and Quantum Physics* by Andrew Zimmerman Jones. June 17, 2017 https://www.thoughtco.com/what-is-a-quantum-computer-2699359

5. *The Age of Spiritual Machines* Ray Kurzweil, author

6. The day wearables replace smartphones http://www.quantumrun.com/prediction/day-wearables-replace-smartphones-future-internet-p5

7. Quantum computing chips massively accelerate machine-learning http://www.quantumrun.com/article/quantum-computing-chips-massively-accelerate-machine-learning

8. Contact lenses into computer screens, February 4, 2016 by Michele Nardelli https://phys.org/news/2016-02-coating-contact-lenses-screens.html

9. Your future inside the Internet of Things: Future of the Internet P4 http://www.quantumrun.com/prediction/your-future-inside-internet-things-future-internet-p4

10. The future of IBM's Watson computer http://wapo.st/1Xj8fFC

11. The Pace of Technology Adoption is Speeding Up

12. The Pace of Technology Adoption is Speeding Up by Rita Gunther McGrath

13. https://hbr.org/2013/11/the-pace-of-technology-adoption-is-speeding-up

Chapter 4
Robots Are My Friends

1. Industrial Robots History http://www.bing.com/videos/search?q=robots+brief+history&qpvt=robots+brief+history&view=detail&mid=08A8286DC31DBDD9304808A8286DC31DBDD93048&rvsmid=56AC4A93FAA14DA7FBED56AC4A93FAA14DA7FBED&fsscr=0&FORM=VDFSRV

2. *"Robots to replace almost half of jobs over next 20 years"* Jorge Branco, in his article for the Brisbane Times http://www.brisbanetimes.com.au/technology/sci-tech/robots-to-replace-almost-half-of-jobs-over-next-20-years-expert-20150323-1m5oei.html

3. Erik Nrynjolfsson of MIT in the McKinsey's new report This 10 minutes conversation provides you with incredible insight into our future robotics life. http://www.mckinsey.com/Videos/video?vid=2448327716001&plyrid=2399849255001

4. Rise of the machines: Fear robots, not China or Mexico http://money.cnn.com/2017/01/30/news/economy/jobs-china-mexico-automation/?iid=EL

5. The Future of Life Institute about the potential future of WAR https://futureoflife.org/open-letter-autonomous-weapons#signatories

6. The Robots, AI, and Unemployment http://lesswrong.com/lw/hh4/the_robots_ai_and_unemployment_antifaq/

7. Future of IBM Watson, http://wapo.st/1Xj8fFC

Recommended Reading

Chapter 5
Medical Innovation

1. The Cloud Can Help Cure Cancer: Goldman Sachs' Isaac Ro. https://www.youtube.com/watch?v=KqMQqT_Zwb0
2. What is Nanotechnology https://www.thoughtco.com/what-is-nanotechnology-2699053Help Cure Cancer [2:52]
3. Can future heart attacks be prevented? Science & medicine race the clock http://www.quantumrun.com/article/can-future-heart-attacks-be-prevented-science-medicine-race-clock
4. Andrew Zimmerman Jones researcher for the ThoughtCo.
5. https://www.thoughtco.com/what-is-nanotechnology-2699053
6. Nanotechnology and Future Energy Generation, Storage and Use https://www.azonano.com/nanotechnology-video-details.aspx?VidID=58
7. 7 Amazing Ways Nanotechnology Is Changing The World By Rebecca Boyle
8. https://www.popsci.com/science/article/2012-11/7-amazing-ways-nanotechnologychanging-world
9. Stem Cells Discovered to be The Superheroes of Healing, which You May Now Utilize!
10. —Dr. Ronald P. Drucker
11. http://drrondrucker.com/blog/2017/05/18/stem-cells-have-emerged-as-the-newsuperheroes-of-healing-which-you-may-now-utilize/

Chapter 6
The Future of Transportation

1. *"Airbus Unveils a Flying Car Concept"* http://robbreport.com/aviation/airbus-unveils-flying-car-concept
2. Finding other habitable planets in the universe http://www.quantumrun.com/article/finding-other-habitable-planets-universe
3. Driverless Bus are closer than you think http://www.quantumrun.com/article/driverless-buses-future
4. Google Unveils New Self Driving Car http://www.quantumrun.com/article/google-unveils-new-self-driving-car
5. Nasa tests 'impossible' engine that could carry passengers to the moon in just four hours http://www.dailymail.co.uk/sciencetech/article-3063082/Has-Nasa-built-WARP-DRIVE-Engineers-claim-tested-impossible-engine-travel-faster-speed-light.html#ixzz502HTpmaj
6. Video of Michael Ronen electric autonomous cars, and how auto ownership is changing http://www.goldmansachs.com/our-thinking/pages/auto-2.0.html
7. Video regarding Lithium Batteries is the new gasoline. http://www.goldmansachs.com/our-thinking/pages/what-if-i-told-you-full/?videoId=143955
8. New Flying Car is more than a concept https://www.bing.com/videos/search?q=Flying+Cars+of+the+Future&&view=detail&mi d=39E6C4A54C7DDE13BACD39E6C4A54C7DDE13BACD&&FORM=VDRVRV
9. 39 Day Mission to Mars http://www.quantumrun.com/article/39-day-mission-mars
10. Autonomous passenger drones are not Sci-Fi anymore http://www.quantumrun.com/article/autonomous-passenger-drones-are-not-sci-fi-anymore
11. Vision of an Autonomous Future https://www.intel.com/content/www/us/en/automotive/autonomousvehicles.html?cid=sem43700027881807471&intel_term=%2Bautomated+%2Bcars&utm_source=bing&utm_medium=cpc&utm_campaign=IntelB2B%

5EPPC%5EUS%5EEN%5EAutonomousDriving%
5EBMM_Bing&utm_term=%2Bautomated%20%
2Bcars&utm_content=autonomous&gclid=CKm
MqreixtcCFcjYDQodjnoDHg&gclsrc=ds

12. The big business future behind self-driving cars: Future of Transportation P2 http://www.quantumrun.com/prediction/big-business-future-behind-self-driving-cars-future-transportation-p2

13. Space is the New Frontier Video http://www.goldmansachs.com/our-thinking/pages/what-if-i-told-you-full/index.html?videoId=141043

14. How Hyperloop Technology Will Enable Us to Reach 760 MPH Speeds http://moneyinc.com/hyperloop-technology-will-enable-us-reach-760-mph-speeds/

15. China is developing a hypersonic space plane that makes the Space Shuttle look primitive https://www.digitaltrends.com/cool-tech/china-space-plane-hypersonic/

16. Tony Seba: Clean Disruption - Energy & Transportation https://www.youtube.com/watch?v=2b3ttqYDwF0&feature=youtu.be

Chapter 7
Departments of Energy

1. China Becomes "Clean Energy Powerhouse" http://online. wsj.com/ad/article/chinaenergy-powerhouse
2. New crystal allows divers to stay underwater for hours http:// www.quantumrun.com/article/scientists-develop-crystal-can-store-massive-amounts-oxygen
3. Scientists are creating an artificial Sun to develop renewable energy http://www.msn.com/en-us/news/technology/scientists-are-creating-an-artificial-sun-to-develop-renewable-energy/ar-BByIAtl?ocid=UE07DHP
4. Global Energy Strategist, *Oil & Energy Investor* Dr. Kent Moors, Battery Breakthough https://moneymorning.com/2017/10/23/the-possible-holy-grail-of-battery-breakthroughs-courtesy-of-mit/
5. The Alternative Energy Sources of the Future http://www. visualcapitalist.com/alternative-energy-sources-future/
6. Fusion energy power stations to fuel our future cities http:// www.quantumrun.com/article/fusion-energy-may-soon-be-used-small-scale-power-stations
7. Opinion: Can technology solve climate change? A Greener Life, A Greener World https://agreenerlifeagreenerworld. net/2016/12/19/opinion-can-technology-solve-climate-change/
8. Lithium is The New Gasoline http://www.goldmansachs.com/ our-thinking/pages/what-if-i-told-you-full/?videoId=143955

Recommended Reading

Chapter 8
Education for Tomorrow

1. The 4 hyperlinks below are for Aptitude Testing that could be the most important test you will ever take.
2. http://yourfreecareertest.com/
3. https://www.whatcareerisrightforme.com/
4. http://www.rasmussen.edu/resources/aptitude-test/
5. http://www.aptitude-test.com/employers/prices.htmlaptitutedest.com
6. Michio Kaku discussess H1B Visas and US Education System https://www.youtube.com/watch?v=Qty1xqvQBrA
7. The World's Leading Nations for Innovation and Technology http://www.citylab.com/tech/2011/10/worlds-leading-nations-innovation-and-technology/224/).
8. Is Graduate School Worth It? By Ellen Hunter Gans Posted in: College & Education http://www.moneycrashers.com/is-grad-school-worth-it/
9. Futuristic Speaker, Thomas Frey By 2030 over 50% of Colleges will Collapse http://www.futuristspeaker.com/business-trends/by-2030-over-50-of-colleges-will-collapse/
10. How to Write a Great Resume for a Job – Tips & Examples, By Kristia Ludwick http://www.moneycrashers.com/write-job-resume-tips-examples/
11. Benefits of Attending Community College for Two Years to Save Money https://www.moneycrashers.com/benefits-of-community-college/
12. 8 digital life skills all children need – and a plan for teaching them https://www.weforum.org/agenda/2016/09/8-digital-life-skills-all-children-need-and-a-plan-for-teaching-them
13. Google exec, Mark Cuban agree that these college majors are the most robot-resistant https://www.cnbc.com/2017/04/21/these-college-majors-are-the-most-robot-resistant.html?_source=msn|money|inline|story|&par=msn&doc=104754806
14. Video about computer programing from the experts https://www.bing.com/videos/search?q=What+School+

Don%27t+Teach+About+Money&&view=detail&mid=13A359089EA4822CDA7613A359089EA4822CDA76&FORM=VRDGAR

15. A nationwide nonprofit corporation that administers and evaluates aptitude test that I highly recommend. (www.jocrf.org),

16. Mark Cuban's Adviseto Highschoolers and College Grads http://www.bing.com/videos/search?q=career+recommendations+to+my+grandson&qpvt=career+recommendations+to+my+grandson&view=detail&mid=FE7BC53E2317CFB81091FE7BC53E2317CFB81091&rvsmid=9C24D8BC20369DF873F49C24D8BC20369DF873F4&fsscr=0&FORM=VDFSRV

17. Aptitude test that can start you off on the right foot .http://www.oprah.Com/omagazine/Aptitude-Tests-Career-Assessment

18. Career Aptitude Test http://yourfreecareertest.com/

19. Career Aptitude Test https://www.whatcareerisrightforme.com/

20. Rassmussen College Aptitude Test http://www.rasmussen.edu/resources/aptitude-test/

21. Aptitude Test http://www.aptitude-test.com/employers/prices.html aptitutedest.com

22. US didn't crack the top 10, by Abby Jackson & Andy Kiersz of Business Insider http://www.businessinsider.com/pisa-worldwide-ranking-of-math-science-reading-skills-2016-12

23. Why the STEM gender gap is overblown and attempts to discredit above article http://www.pbs.org/newshour/making-sense/truth-women-stem-careers/

Chapter 9

Help Wanted

1. The AI Revolution http://banyanhill.com/the-ai-revolution/
2. The Booming Demand for Commercial Drone Pilots by Tiffany Kelly https://www.theatlantic.com/technology/archive/2017/01/drone-pilot-school/515022/
3. Amazon is creating 100,000 U.S. jobs, but at what cost? Jon Swartz, USA TODAY https://www.usatoday.com/story/tech/columnist/2017/01/13/amazons-jobs-creation-plan-comes-amid-labor-pains/96488166/
4. Lower Wages for American Workers http://www.fairus.org/issue/lower-wages-for-american-workers
5. 11 experts at Davos on the future of work https://www.weforum.org/agenda/2016/01/11-experts-at-davos-on-the-future-of-work
6. Four changes shaping the labor market https://www.weforum.org/agenda/2016/01/four-changes-shaping-the-labour-market
7. Is the future of work a man's world? 3 ways women can win. This article present the hard facts and ways women can protect themselves https://www.weforum.org/agenda/2017/01/future-of-jobs-women-female-automation
8. AI, Robotics, and the Future of Jobs, by Aaron Smith and Janna Anderson of Pew Research Center http://www.pewinternet.org/2014/08/06/FUTURE-OF-JOBS/
9. Best Computer Jobs for the Future, by Daniel Greenpan http://www.itcareerfinder.com/brain-food/blog/entry/best-computer-jobs-for-the-future.html
10. The TPP: More Job Offshoring and Lower Wages (Trans-Pacific-Partnership) http://www.citizen.org/documents/tpp-wages-jobs.pdf
11. VIDEO: President Obama responds to wife of unemployed Engineer who was replaced by H-1B program https://youtu.be/K_CMXLBd17k
12. H-1B Visa video https://www.youtube.com/watch?v=Qty1xqvQBrA

13. A student who worked in a Chinese iPhone factory explains why manufacturing jobs aren't coming back http://www.msn.com/en-us/money/markets/a-student-who-worked-in-a-chinese-iphone-factory-explains-why-manufacturing-jobs-arent-coming-back/ar-BBAyp2Q?li=BBnb7Kz&ocid=UE07DHP

14. The future of American jobs lies with the tech industry by <u>Abinash Tripathy</u>

15. https://techcrunch.com/2017/01/27/the-future-of-american-jobs-lies-with-the-tech-industry/

16. The Jobless Future Is Coming by Michael Robinson, Strategic Tech Investor http://strategictechinvestor.com/special-reports-video/the-jobless-future-is-coming/

17. The Reality of Drones for Private Industry http://www.quantumrun.com/article/reality-drones-private-enterprise

18. Drones take over $127 Billion in jobs from humans http://moneyinc.com/drones-take-127-billion-humans-2020/

19. Generation Jobless: The Unemployment Crisis of Millennials http://www.fairus.org/publications/generation-jobless

20. 10 Future Technology Jobs That Will Exist in 10 Years But Don't Now http://moneyinc.com/future-technology-jobs/

21. Is technology eliminating jobs at a faster rate than they are being created? https://www.quora.com/Is-technology-eliminating-jobs-at-a-faster-rate-than-they-are-being-created

22. Surprisingly, These 10 Professional Jobs Are Under Threat From Big Data https://www.google.com/amp/www.forbes.com/sites/bernardmarr/2016/04/25/surprisingly-these-10-professional-jobs-are-under-threat-from-big-data/amp/?client=safari

23. Technology has created more jobs than it has destroyed, says 140 years of data https://www.theguardian.com/business/2015/aug/17/technology-created-more-jobs-than-destroyed-140-years-data-census

24. The jobs of the future — and two skills you need to get them https://www.weforum.org/agenda/2016/09/jobs-of-future-and-skills-you-need

25. The Future of Jobs http://reports.weforum.org/future-of-jobs-2016/

Recommended Reading

26. Jobs are created by advancement in the computers. https://www.theatlantic.com/business/archive/2016/01/automation-paradox/424437/

27. The Future of Jobs and Skills http://www3.weforum.org/docs/WEF_FOJ_Executive_Summary_Jobs.pdf

28. Does your job title matter anymore? https://www.weforum.org/agenda/2016/01/future-skills/

29. The job for life model is dead. Here's what millennials need to knowhttps://www.weforum.org/agenda/2016/06/how-to-get-the-most-out-of-millennial-workers-teach-them-new-skills

30. Surviving your future workplace: Future of Work http://www.quantumrun.com/prediction/surviving-your-future-workplace-future-work-p1

31. 2 Billion Jobs to Disappear by 2030 http://www.futuristspeaker.com/business-trends/2-billion-jobs-to-disappear-by-2030/

32. https://money.usnews.com/careers/best-jobs/rankings/the-100-best-jobs

33. http://clark.com/employment-military/10-best-future-jobs/

34. http://www.collegerank.net/best-careers-for-the-future/

35. Best Jobs for the Future, *Money Watch* https://www.cbsnews.com/news/best-jobs-for-the-future/

36. Best Jobs of the Future *Kiplinger* https://www.kiplinger.com/slideshow/business/T012-S001-best-jobs-for-the-future-2017/index.html

37. Best Jobs that Don't Require a College Degree from *Kiplinger* https://www.kiplinger.com/slideshow/business/T012-S001-best-jobs-without-a-college-degree-2017/index.html

38. Best Construction Jobs https://money.usnews.com/careers/best-jobs/rankings/best-construction-jobs

39. Best Creative and Media Jobs https://money.usnews.com/careers/best-jobs/rankings/best-creative-and-media-jobs

40. Best Education Jobs https://money.usnews.com/careers/best-jobs/rankings/best-education-jobs

41. Best Engineering Jobs https://money.usnews.com/careers/best-jobs/rankings/best-engineering-jobs

42. Best Health Care Jobs https://money.usnews.com/careers/best-jobs/rankings/best-healthcare-jobs

Morgan

43. Best Health Care Support Jobs https://money.usnews.com/careers/best-jobs/rankings/best-health-care-support-jobs

44. Best Maintenance and Repair Jobs https://money.usnews.com/careers/best-jobs/rankings/best-maintenance-and-repair-jobs

45. Best Sales and Marketing Jobs https://money.usnews.com/careers/best-jobs/rankings/best-sales-and-marketing-jobs

46. Best Science Jobs https://money.usnews.com/careers/best-jobs/rankings/best-science-jobs

47. Best Social Services Jobs https://money.usnews.com/careers/best-jobs/rankings/best-social-services-jobs

48. Best Technology Jobs https://money.usnews.com/careers/best-jobs/rankings/best-technology-jobs

49. Occupational Outlook Handbook https://www.bls.gov/ooh/occupation finder.htm?pay=$75,000+or+more&education=Bachelor%E2%80%99s+degree&training=None&newjobs=50,000+or+more&growth=Much+faster+than+average&submit=GO

50. US New & World Report 100 Best Jobs https://money.usnews.com/careers/bestjobs/rankings/the-100-best-jobs

51. Top 10 Best Jobs for the Future. http://clark.com/employment-military/10-best-future-jobs/

52. 10 Best Careers for the Future from College Rank http://www.collegerank.net/best-careers-for-the-future/

53. **The Bureau of Labor Statistics**[47] -Occupational Outlook, Highest paying & Fastest growing https://www.bls.gov/ooh/

54. Careers to Explore – STEM CAREERS https://www.bls.gov/spotlight/2017/science-technology-engineering-and-mathematics-stem-occupations-past-present-and-future/pdf/science-technology-engineering-and-mathematics-stem-occupations-past-present-and-future.pd

Recommended Reading

123

Chapter 10
People, Politics, and Problems

1. Mark Lautman,, an Economic Developer, in his book *"When the Boomers Bail: A Community Economic Survival Guide*

2. Should You Be Worried About How Artificial Intelligence Will Affect the Economy?https://www.forbes.com/sites/northwesternmutual/2017/02/28/should-you-be-worried-about-how-artificial-intelligence-will-affect-the-economy/#1e16124cb26c

3. The future of military cloaking devices http://www.quantumrun.com/article/future-military-cloaking-devices

4. Drones set to Transform Future Police Work http://www.quantumrun.com/article/role-domestic-drones-future-police-work

5. Future e-waste will destroy itself http://www.quantumrun.com/article/future-your-e-waste-will-destroy-itself

6. These 12 technologies will drive our economic future By Neil Irwin https://www.washingtonpost.com/news/wonk/wp/2013/05/24/these-12-technologies-will-drive-our-economic-future/?utm_term=.952f3a4b5f3e

7. The Cost of Living is poised to plummet "technological socialism" https://www.google.com/amp/s/singularityhub.com/2016/07/18/why-the-cost-of-living-is-poised-to-plummet-in-the-next-20-years/amp/?client=safari

8. Rich and poor teenagers use the web differently – here's what this is doing to inequality https://www.weforum.org/agenda/2016/07/rich-and-poor-teenagers-spend-a-similar-amount-of-time-online-so-why-aren-t-we-closing-the-digital-divide/

9. Future of climate change http://www.quantumrun.com/series/future-climate-change-0#start-here

10. House price crisis and underground housing alternative http://www.quantumrun.com/article/house-price-crisis-and-underground-housing-alternative

Morgan

11. Urban Future http://www.quantumrun.com/prediction/our-future-urban-future-cities-p1
12. Mega Cities of Tomorrow http://www.quantumrun.com/prediction/planning-megacities-tomorrow-future-cities-p2
13. Density-based City property taxes http://www.quantumrun.com/prediction/density-tax-revolution-property-taxes-will-kill-climate-change
14. New tools to rebuild and replace infrastructure http://www.quantumrun.com/prediction/infrastructure-rebuilding-megacities-future-cities-p6

Chapter 11
Me, Myself, and I

1. InnoCentive Innovation is the most independent, 3rd Party, incentivized, advance problem solving technique ever to be developed and is exploding with solutions for any business. https://cdn2.hubspot.net/hubfs/2245722/EBooks/ebook%20general%20v1.4.pdf?__hssc=253935447.1.1 512392287554&__hstc=253935447.032db4042a862721 24642183245c91b9.1507722040182.1508602086713.15123 92287554.4&__hsfp=3216665191&hsCtaTracking=999ee6 ac-11fc-43ad-8f6e-6804482c44ba%7C4a1a28b7-c7ef-4484-89e2-6c6a043781c9

2. https://www.innocentive.com/?utm_campaign=Nurture%20 -%203%20Stage%20Follow%20Up%20Emails&utm_ source=hs_automation&utm_medium=email&utm_ content=54967314&_hsenc=p2ANqtz-9opeeVHY7lzDpXroPvooU_x7eNCezlTPkJg2izxMacq_zT 4qkdseyRfzAUE66MAKGjal71GmiC0h7mueh tP-4WCSmFgcrQhWrs22acFMCe_SdoucM&_ hsmi=54967314#home-page-video

3. 10 Wildly Successful Startups and Lessons to Learn From Them http://www.inc.com/dave-kerpen/10-wildly-successful-startups-and-lessons-to-learn-from-them.html

4. YCombinator support for start-up companies http://www.ycombinator.com/

5. 6 Female Entrepreneurs than built their fortune from Scratch https://www.investopedia.com/financial-edge/0611/6-female-entrepreneurs-who-built-their-fortunes-from-scratch.aspx#ixzz4nJd7VzXn

6. The Best Way to Play Tech Stocks in 2017 https://money morning.com/2017/05/04/the-best-way-to-play-tech-stocks-in-2017/

7. 9 successful Tech Entrepreneurs Stories https://www. entrepreneur.com/slideshow/225816#4

8. https://www.entrepreneur.com/slideshow/225816#0

Morgan

9. Hall Of Fame Famous & Successful Entrepreneurs List http://thelittlee.com/html/famous_entrepreneurs.html

10. Intuit/Docstoc Sale $50 Million Acquisition http://allthingsd.com/20131204/intuit-buys-docstoc-for-up-to-50-million-to-round-out-small-business-services/

11. 16 Surprising Statistics About Small Businesses https://www.forbes.com/sites/jasonnazar/2013/09/09/16-surprising-statistics-about-small-businesses/#1e028f885ec8

12. The gig economy is changing the way we work. Now regulation must catch up https://www.weforum.org/agenda/2016/06/gig-economy-changing-work

13. Farewell, job title. Hello, skill set https://www.weforum.org/agenda/2016/06/the-benefits-of-looking-beyond-job-titles

14. The Future of the Professions: How Technology Will Transform the Work of Human Experts by Richard Susskind https://www.goodreads.com/work/quotes/43048877-the-future-of-the-professions-how-technology-will-transform-the-work-of

15. Youngest Self Made Female Billionaire https://www.bing.com/videos/search?q=what+they+don%27t+teach+you+in+high+school&qpvt=what+they+don%27t+teach+you+in+high+school&view=detail&mid=F72FDBD6B6A5A9F10F4FF72FDBD6B6A5A9F10F4F&&FORM=VDRVRV

16. Additionally, an entrepreneurial company out of Baltimore Maryland, BluePrint Robotics http://www.blueprint-robotics.com/video/

17. Housing prices crash as 3D printing and maglevs revolutionize construction: Future of Cities P3http://www.quantumrun.com/prediction/housing-prices-crash-3d-printing-and-maglevs-revolutionize-construction-future-cities-p3

18. Rapid construction https://www.youtube.com/watch?v=veNf-bz99cI

19. Contour Crafting: How 3D Printing Will Change Construction http://www.popularmechanics.com/technology/infrastructure/a10342/contour-crafting-how-3d-printing-will-change-construction-16594743/

20. Better data saves marine mammals http://www.quantumrun.com/article/better-data-saves-marine-mammals

Recommended Reading

127

21. Urban World http://www.mckinsey.com/global-themes/urbanization/urban-world-cities-and-the-rise-of-the-consuming-class

22. Housing Construction with Robots. http://www.blueprint-robotics.com/video

23. The Future of Urban Housing https://www.houselogic.com/remodel/future-urban-housing/

24. The Impact of Technology on Living Environments for Older Adults https://www.ncbi.nlm.nih.gov/books/NBK97336/?report=classic

25. Animation of Contour Crafting in whole house construction (high res) https://www.youtube.com/watch?v=M_LLSsNnHn8&hl=en%5FUS&version=3

26. Real Estate Costs in Megacities Can't Go Up Forever: Tyler Cowen http://nreionline.com/investment/real-estate-costs-megacities-cant-go-forever-tyler-cowen?NL=NREI-21&Issue=NREI-21_20170324_NREI-21_750&sfvc4enews=42&cl=article_5_b&utm_rid=CPG09000005670194&utm_campaign=8879&utm_medium=email&elq2=12372c2678734b289c4fe76a20dc19df

27. Commercial Real Estate 25 page report from Deloitte outlining innovations https://www2.deloitte.com/content/dam/Deloitte/us/Documents/Real%20Estate/us-innovations-in-commercial-real-estate.pdf

Chapter 12
Love Really Does Make the World Go 'Round

Chapter 13
Back From the Future

1. The AI Revolution http://banyanhill.com/the-ai-revolution/
2. Washington Post Technology Trends and Economic Impact https://www.washingtonpost.com/news/wonk/wp/2013/ 05/24/these-12-technologies-will-drive-our-economic- future/?utm_term=.952f3a4b5f3e
3. The 6 Jobs Everyone Will Want in 2040 http://www.msn.com/ en-us/money/careersandeducation/the-6-jobs-everyone-will- want-in-2040/ar-AAtD2lN?li=BBnb7Kz&ocid=UE07DHP
4. Greatest Scientist in the world https://www.thoughtco.com/ most-influential-scientists-in-20th-century-1779904
5. 33 Dramatic Predictions for 2030 http://www.futuristspeaker. com/business-trends/33-dramatic-predictions-for-2030/
6. *Vacant and Abandoned Properties: Turning Liabilities Into Assets* https://www.huduser.gov/portal/periodicals/em/winter14/ highlight1.html

John **Morgan** Mullen previously has written *Kernels of Knowledge* that creatively provides a mental road map that teaches its readers how to crawl inside your head and walks you through a process designed to determine "where you are", "where you want to go", and "how you get there." It utilizes thought provoking and sometimes humorous quotes, a pinch of life stories, a dash of poetry, and two parts practical and proven advice. It delves into the creative power of thoughts and dreams and how, when carefully harnessed, you can eliminate your fears, define your goals and, through persistence and coordinate effort can make your dreams come true. There is a fine line between insanity and brilliance as you crawl inside your head and not only talk, but sometimes debate with your own internal experts. This 1st Chapter of *Kernels of Knowledge* (*"Meetings with Myself"*), presented here walks you through the baby steps that will lead you from thoughts to dreams, from dreams to action steps, and action steps to your reality.

Kernels of Knowledge

Change Your Thinking, Change Your Life

By: Morgan

Meetings with Myself

A few years back, I created a self-evaluation system based on the following questions: "Where am I?" "Where do I want to go?" and "What do I have to do to get there?" Answer these three questions and dedicate yourself to the achievement of these goals, and you will be happy for the rest of your life. My "Meetings with Myself" were always interesting and entertaining; they allowed me to evaluate whether I was moving in the right direction. It's one of those mind games that are best performed alone.

"Find a place of solitude. Look into the distance, and into the future. Visualize the tomorrow you are going to build; and begin to build that tomorrow, today."–Jonathan Lockwood Huie

You might want to sit in a yoga position, with legs crossed and palms open, and give in to the energy around you. Or you might want to do what I do—just relax, make yourself comfortable, and get ready for an enlightening journey. Turn off the computers and the iPhone, as you will be going to a place that they can never understand. Find a quiet place, relax, and take yourself into your fantasy world, surrounded with silence and peace, away from your chaotic life. Music is optional.

Man is a slow, sloppy and brilliant thinker; the machine is fast, accurate and stupid. ~William M. Kelly

As Rhonda Byrne writes in her book The Secret, the law of attraction indicates you can control what you think and believe. I do not presume to understand how the mind works; however, if you are able to tap into this power of your inner thoughts and learn to control what you think, then you can better direct and control not only what happens in your life but also the results. I'm not sure that "If I believe, if I just think it," it will magically happen—I'm just a kid from Ohio who used to play football. So when we start talking about "visualizations," "inner seeing," and vibrations that are transferred into the atmosphere, I get a little lost. But what I do know and adamantly support is that if you believe in your thoughts and focus on those things you need to change, you can make it happen. If you can learn to control and formulate what you think in a logical sequence and transfer those thoughts into your dreams and actions, then anything is possible.

What we are today comes from our thoughts of yesterday,
and our present thoughts build our lives of tomorrow.

—Buddha

This Meeting with Myself exercise is independent, unabashed, and uncensored. It has a few rules and boundaries that allow for truthful self-evaluation of where you are, where you want to go, and how best to achieve those goals. The entire process is designed around careful and creative thoughts and dreams.

You have the power to control your mind, to visualize, and to evaluate. This allows you to look inside your head and plant the seeds of thoughts and dreams that, when cultivated, can define, grow, and provide you direction.

The mind is a powerful ally of the brain. Your brain is your own built-in three-pound computer, made up of 100 billion neurons that regulates all physical aspects of your body—from heartbeat to blood pressure, from nerves to breathing, from taste to smell. Your mind, however, is not limited to physical functions; it also encompasses the emotional power within you.

Dr. Daniel Siegel, a professor of psychiatry at UCLA School of Medicine, in his book, Mindsight: The New Science of Personal Transformation, identifies the relationship between our brains and our minds as a "powerful lens through which we can understand our inner lives with more clarity, integrate the brain, and enhance our relationships with others. Mindsight is a kind of focused attention that allows us to see the internal workings of our own minds. It helps us get ourselves off of the autopilot of ingrained behaviors and habitual responses. It lets us 'name and tame' the emotions we are experiencing, rather than being overwhelmed by them."

Dr. Siegel dispels the notion of the old saying "Talking with yourself is OK so long as you don't talk back." You can call it whatever you want— meditation, self-talk, or Meetings with Myself—but this all-important journey through your mind helps formulate your direction and crystallizes your plans.

Recommended Reading

137

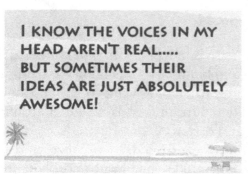

He who knows others is wise;
he who knows himself is enlightened.

—Lao Tzu, Chinese author

Psychologists indicate that talking with yourself is perfectly normal and can have a great deal of emotional benefit that contradicts the idea "What can we tell ourselves that we don't already know?" It helps to focus and clarify your thoughts and evaluate and confirm your decisions. Dr. Charles Chio states in his article published in Live Science magazine, "Talking to Yourself may Boost Brainpower", indicates that "Talking to yourself might not mean you are crazy—it can actually benefit thinking and perception." It's always beneficial to talk through your problem by having a serious dialogue with yourself in the privacy of your own mind, and be sure to consult with all of the voices in your head, your own mental board of directors—the dreamer, the accountant, the pessimist, the deal junkie, the marketing person, the lawyer, and whoever else has been invited to your meeting.

Your inner voice is subtle
but grows stronger when you listen.

—Unknown

Morgan

138

Your meetings have only a few rules:

1. Find a quiet place.
2. Do not allow any interruptions.
3. Take only brief notes to avoid disruptions of the creative process.

These conversations will be documented and incorporated into your game plan in chapter 2.

The sequence of the questions is important, as you need to know your starting point prior to attempting to establish where you want to go. You would think that determining "How do I get there?" would be the most difficult question; however, you will learn that "Where do I want to go?" actually requires the most imagination, is the most difficult to visualize, and is the most important to your success. It entails looking inside your soul to determine what you want to do when you grow up—a tall order. Growing up is when you take that first step into our new world and find out who you are, lose the illusions of youth, and discover the world of choices. There is no predetermined age that this miracle is discovered; it might be twenty or forty...or never.

When work, commitment, and pleasure all become one and you reach that deep well where passion lives, nothing is impossible.

—Anonymous

This exercise requires passion, assessment, and concentration, with a dash of realism. Once the "where" becomes evident, the "how" is easier to identify, schedule, and achieve.

If you don't know where you want to go, most any road will get you there.

—Lewis Carroll, English author of Alice's Adventures in Wonderland

Recommended Reading

WHERE AM I?

"Where am I?" generally takes the stage first. Evaluate each of the projects or relationships you are involved with, and recap the issues and decisions you've made, as well as any changes that you were required to implement. You must look in the mirror and deal with your current realities. The "Where am I?" agenda is a review of your current situation and entails more of an administrative review or highlight of the existing facts—what you have been able to accomplish and why, along with what your pending issues are and their current statuses.

WHERE DO I WANT TO GO?

The "Where do I want to go?" follows this evaluation. This is the most fun and also the most important of all your objectives. You need to realize that in order for this session to truly be productive, you need to tell the pessimist in you to sit down and shut up—he or she will never believe your dreams are possible. I also like to make sure the "deal junkie" is in attendance, as he or she believe you can fly. This is your time to dream, and in your dream world, you can achieve anything you can conceive. While the pessimist's opinions are extremely important, he or she can rejoin you later and bring all his or her input in the "How do I get there?" session.

Vision is the art of seeing things invisible.

—Jonathan Swift, Anglo-Irish poet

It's important to raise the bar, to dream, and to picture yourself living in the world you wish to build. There are no boundaries; you are limited only by your imagination. Your career, love life, car, house, or money—it's all on the table. This session requires uninhibited imagination. In most cases, you might find that you hesitate to allow yourself to attempt to achieve your dreams and goals for fear of failure. You need to set those fears aside and just go for it!

It helps if you ask yourself where you want to be in one year, in five years, or even in ten years. It's difficult to determine the answer to "Where do I want to go?" but it's imperative that you do so. Evaluating the probabilities should be minimized, as you do not want to limit or discourage, but rather set yourself free to dream the impossible. Those negative thoughts will destroy the continuity of this session and will be discussed later in detail during the "How do I get there?" session. Be crystal clear as to your vision, dedicate yourself, and have belief in your ability to achieve it. Deadlines, obstacles, and roadblocks to achievement will all be evaluated later. Now is your time to dream. And never, ever let your fears prevent you from living your dream life.

The greater danger for most of us is not that our aim is too high and we miss it, but that it is too low and we reach it.

—Michelangelo

I recently read an interesting article called "The Second Wave of Transformation," by John Mauldin. He outlines several compelling projections of how technology will change our lives in the next two decades, and we need to be aware of these changes and incorporate them into our future planning. One of Mr. Mauldin's intriguing projections, which is near and dear to our hearts, states, "We won't be physically immortal, but the things that kill most of us today will not be a problem. We will just get…older. And we will be able to repair a great deal of the damage from aging." Scientists are even "starting to print 3-D human organs," according to the article, and Mauldin also purports that "we will see more change in the next twenty years than we saw in the last one hundred!"

So the good news is that maybe—just maybe—you will live longer than you thought, but the bad news is that if you are not prepared, your financial world could be a disaster. As Michelangelo stated, "it might be better to aim too high and miss than aim too low and make it." It's important to keep this in mind and incorporate it into your "Where do I want to go?" and "How do I get there?" sessions.

We should also be aware that this session was researched by the "accountant." He or she understands that in the 1960s, there were one hundred thousand millionaires. It has been projected, however, that by the mid-twenty-first century, all professionals will be millionaires, according to observations by Burleson Consulting

Recommended Reading

141

(www.burlesonconsulting.com). The percentage of millionaires in the United States will have increased from 3 percent of the population in 2007 (nine million) to approximately 20 percent of the population by 2050 (seventy million). Now, a loaf of bread might cost twenty dollars in 2050, but what this tells you is that you might want to raise the bar, because your financial world is changing. You need to take these facts into consideration in your Meetings with Myself.

Your Meetings with Myself is not a one-time process, but rather a continual exercise that should be scheduled periodically. In most cases, "Where do I want to go?" has been discussed and established early on, in previous meetings, as this is essential to your direction and affects the establishment of directional task from the onset; however, these objectives need to be continually revisited and updated as required. But more importantly, you need to continually reinforce your dreams and constantly monitor your progress.

HOW DO I GET THERE?

Finally we have the all-important "How do I get there?" session. Occasionally, you're required to make changes, and as author of your dream thoughts, you reserve the right and responsibility to initiate these adjustments as needed. Written synopsis, incorporated in the game plan in the next chapter, is essential, or you can get lost. The very acts of writing down your goal, formulating your plan, and transferring its steps to your to-do list embed in your mind the direction and guarantee the actions required to keep you on track to accomplish your goals.

You don't make decisions in a vacuum; they require input from those internal and external experts who have dealt with the issues, those who know the people and problems and deal with them every day. Healthy conflicts are inevitable—say, between the ego person in you, who wants to buy that big house, and the accountant in you, who says, "You're an idiot" (those unabashed, uncensored discussions we have within our minds).

Now, it's true you are talking with yourself—and some may view this as being a little crazy—but within us all, we have those bits of expertise that we call upon periodically when evaluating how we need to get where we want to go. For example, depending on the problem you are evaluating, you might recall the experience of the marketing person or the lawyer or the one I hate—the accountant—for inspiration prior to making decisions and formulating your plan.

Now, you may think this self-talk is a little crazy—and maybe it is, but you need to remember there is a thin line between brilliance and insanity.

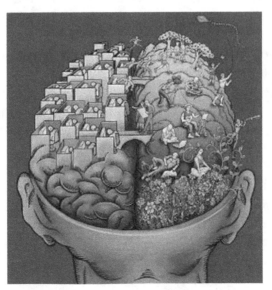

The point is that your mind and experiences allow you to evaluate the steps you need to take to determine the direction you have to go before implementing your best plan. Experience has taught us that

Recommended Reading

while it's not a lot of fun talking with the accountant, as a general rule, he or she needs to sign off on all financial matters incorporated into the final plan.

Now, sometimes you make decisions on the spur of the moment, and sometimes that works. I'm just saying that decisions will work better and be successful more often if you have thought about them first. You can make better decisions with better results if you debate them before your board of directors.

The "How do I get there?" meeting requires that each thought be developed into specific goals and steps that require action, so set the beer down, and let's get to work. This is where the rubber meets the road. All those grand plans can't be achieved without documenting and setting time frames for those tasks, ones that clearly describe "How do I get there?"

You have crawled inside your head, and only you can clearly define those goals you have set up for yourself. It reminds me of a story about a project manager who was talking with one of his ambitious, overachieving team members. As he laid out those tasks that needed to be done, the overachiever continually answered, "I can do that!" to all the assignments. But later, after the meeting, in the quiet of his own office, the team member said to himself, "Oh, shit. How am I going to do all that?" The same is true with the goals that you've established in the "Where do I want to go?" segment of your meetings. Now you need to determine the "how."

First, you need to clearly articulate to yourself on paper exactly what you have determined your goals to be. If you are like me in the "Where do I want to go?" session, you would have got a little crazy and were carried away. This is when you need to bring in the administration person and call upon his or her expertise to organize all the craziness. In other words, you need to organize your thoughts.

Now, please don't think that the "crazy" I'm talking about is truly crazy, because crazy sits directly on that line between insanity and brilliance. So brilliance or insanity—I don't know, you decide.

This is the time when you, as the chairman of the board, call in all your internal experts. You need to bring back the pessimist, the accountant, the lawyer—the whole team. How you document this is up to you, but my administrative person likes to break it down into two categories: personal (health, relationships, family, friends, self-esteem, respect, attitude, love, freedom, and all the other things money can't buy), and financial (income, house, car, travel, and all the other things money can buy).

I think it's important to realize that happiness and success are not always about money. There are good reasons why "personal" is listed first. The principles outlined in this book are equally transferable to both. Too often we interpret a motivational or a self-help book as dealing primarily with our financial world and secondarily to our health, love, respect, relationships, and self-esteem. Happiness is achieved through a coordinated balance of the two. Being financially secure without good health doesn't work well. To have money without love is empty. Money without family and friends or respect doesn't mean much, either.

A high priority on my list is to play a part in the lives of my children and my grandchildren. A few years ago, I read an inspirational book by Mac Anderson and Lance Wubbels called *To a Child Love Is Spelled T-I-M-E*. It features a story about a father who takes off work to go fishing with his son. Years later, he reads through his daily journals and comes across his note for that day: "Wasted all day…took Johnny fishing, didn't catch anything." He notices he also has Johnny's diary, so he checks to see what Johnny wrote about that day. Johnny's diary reads, "Spent time with Dad, went fishing, and it was the greatest day of my life!" Think about this in establishing the priority of your dreams.

Each goal, whether personal or financial, requires a clear, brief statement as to your objective. Additionally, it requires those specific tasks that are needed to achieve your goals and a time frame for attaining them.

One example of my dream playing a part in the lives of my children and my children's children was when my wife and I established "Kids Camp." Each year, we invite all children, young and old (as we are all kids at heart), to spend the weekend at our Michigan home, playing in the swimming hole, having water wars, stargazing, and holding a fishing contest, fish fry, and corn fest. Besides being a great time, the annual bonding is amazing, and the memories will last forever.

Recommended Reading

Change how a person thinks and you will change how they feel.
Change how they feel, and you will change how they perform.
Change how they perform and you will change the results.
Change the results and you will change their lives"– RW Ross

Your entire game plan evolves as you walk through this process. Sometimes the pessimist is right. Sometimes the accountant will determine that your goal needs refining. Sometimes the doctor is like a broken record telling you, "Lose weight. Lose weight." And sometimes the love of your life breaks your heart.

Your internal experts have their limitations, and in many cases they require outside counsel. The accountant periodically enlists the expertise of a CPA, bank, or investors. The creative person may consult with the professional architect, the constructor may consult with the engineer, and the lawyer may spend a lot of time with the attorney. The "how" requires a continual search for input through and cooperation from the outside world.

"How do I get there?" sometimes requires finding a mentor. Seek advice or sign up for that class that you've been putting off for the last five years. As the Nike ads say, just do it! Don't be afraid to ask for help. Your contact list is a powerful tool. Use it!

I want to tell you a story that I heard from John Lawrence, an author and career counselor. A friend's son asked John for his advice. The young man had been accepted to Harvard and, at the other end of the spectrum, also Ball State University, a small college located in Muncie, Indiana. He was impressed with the idea of a degree from Harvard. However, the cost difference was about $40,000 per year. John's recommendation to this student, who wanted to work in the motion picture business, and his father was: go to Ball State. It has a very good communications department for theater, art, and film. Then, with the money he saved by not going to Harvard, he could spend the entire summer in Los Angeles, working in the film industry as an unpaid intern. This invaluable experience and contacts that would be realized would go a long way in offsetting the prestige of a degree from Harvard.

I guess what I'm saying is that some sort of combination of experience and education is the ultimate goal. Find a way to add to your education and generate contacts that could give you an introduction to the business as well as put you at the front of the line when looking for a job once you graduate. A good mentor is priceless on your journey to finding your dreams.

The evolution of your dreams is continuous, and flexibility is required. The roadmap outlined in the next chapter, "Game Plan," will provide the step-by-step guidelines to take you from where you are to where you want to be. Please understand that, when completed, this becomes the most important document in the world to you, so treat it accordingly.

READ KERNELS OF KNOWLEDGE <u>HERE</u>

Recommended Reading